THE SUNDAY TIMES

Essential Management Accounting

How to maximise profit and boost financial performance

Belinda Steffan

**KOGAN
PAGE**

London and Philadelphia

Publisher's note

Every possible effort has been made to ensure that the information contained in this book is accurate at the time of going to press, and the publishers and author cannot accept responsibility for any errors or omissions, however caused. No responsibility for loss or damage occasioned to any person acting, or refraining from action, as a result of the material in this publication can be accepted by the editor, the publisher or the authors.

First published in Great Britain in 2008 by Kogan Page Limited

Apart from any fair dealing for the purposes of research or private study, or criticism or review, as permitted under the Copyright, Designs and Patents Act 1988, this publication may only be reproduced, stored or transmitted, in any form or by any means, with the prior permission in writing of the publishers, or in the case of reprographic reproduction in accordance with the terms and licences issued by the CLA. Enquiries concerning reproduction outside these terms should be sent to the publishers at the undermentioned address:

120 Pentonville Road
London N1 9JN
United Kingdom
www.kogan-page.co.uk

© Belinda Steffan, 2008

The right of Belinda Steffan to be identified as the author of this work has been asserted by her in accordance with the Copyright, Designs and Patents Act 1988.

The views expressed in this book are those of the author, and are not necessarily the same as those of Times Newspapers Ltd.

British Library Cataloguing in Publication Data

A CIP record for this book is available from the British Library.

ISBN 978 0 7494 5067 0

Typeset by JS Typesetting Ltd, Porthcawl, Mid Glamorgan
Printed and bound in India by Replika Press Pvt Ltd

Contents

Introduction

Small to medium-sized enterprises (SMEs) make up 94 per cent of all business in the UK. SMEs can be simple, yet complex, and can range from two people turning over less than £100k per year to 250 people working to produce a turnover of more than £11m per year. The SME is an important part of the business environment in the UK – important to consumers, other small businesses, to the government and to large multinationals alike.

While the SME forms an integral part of the business community, a relatively low emphasis on corporate governance and financial performance falls on this important group of companies. *Essential Management Accounting* looks to bring the financial tools used by the biggest companies in the UK to the smallest, many of whom would undoubtedly see increased efficiency through the application of basic management accounting techniques.

SMEs can benefit from the same analysis, planning and control tools as large multinational companies. Operating a small company is no excuse for inefficiency. The same business principles apply to SMEs as to larger public companies, so why do we find so many SMEs lacking in basic business infrastructure – such as analysis, controls and planning?

The key driver for any company – large or small, public or private – should be to increase shareholder wealth. Generally, shareholder wealth increases as a result of an increase in retained profits and other activity generating a positive outcome for the company. Of course, there are many other issues by which a company should be run – social, ethical and environmental; however, the directors of a company have a legal obligation to ensure that the increase of shareholder wealth is at the top of their agenda. Public companies have teams of accountants, analysts, planners and audit committees who ensure that such increase in shareholder wealth is upheld.

SMEs, however, generally do not have the luxury of such support functions owing to lack of working capital for non-core activities. As a result, management tend to focus on core activities. I'll be the first to agree that this is essential for an SME; however, I would also remind managers that their obligation to be as profitable and as successful as possible is no lesser than for larger and more cash-rich entities. Through the application of basic management accounting techniques, the owner/manager of an SME can apply techniques that can streamline and improve the profitability of their business without the requirement for the expensive, highly skilled professional labour of a much larger company.

So, how can management accounting be applied, by the business manager, to the business to improve efficiency and profitability? Management accounting is more than just accounting and more than just management. In fact, as you work your way through the book you'll notice that just a small percentage of the content relates to traditional 'accounting'. The management techniques applied look at how the whole company works within itself and its commercial environment and then drills down to specific areas to ensure that maximum efficiency is achieved and maintained. It's amazing how an improvement in information systems can ultimately lead to increased profitability.

The two principles upon which this book relies are: 1) all business areas are interlinked; and 2) all business areas are linked to the profitability of the company. As an accountant, I have often had people from other departments ask me why I am 'interfering' with areas like marketing, human resources (HR), legal or information technology (IT). The fact of the matter is that all business areas make up a common company and all business areas should be driven to maximum efficiency, which means working together as resourcefully and professionally as possible. People tend to get quite protective of their own tasks within a company and fail to see the big picture.

Let's look at the areas we'll be covering in the book before we move on to analyse how they interact with each other.

Part 1 Business planning and analysis

1 Business planning

The importance of correct and timely planning of a business is critical to its future. Management accounting techniques allow the business owner to project sales, profits, cashflow and market trends, upon which important business decisions can be made to capitalise on opportunities as they arise.

2 Working capital management

Cash is king in a start-up just as it is with a mature business. Working capital management relates to improving cashflow through the effective use of debtors, creditors and other controllable cash movements. The application of the methods to free up capital to work for the business will allow more flexibility and options for business management.

3 Marketing

Marketing is a massive area of expertise that can often intimidate the small business owner. It can be easy to market your product and company well, provided the appropriate amount of research into geography and demographics has been carried out. An explanation of the use of the 'Four Ps' (price, product, promotion and placement), known as the 'marketing mix', will set up businesses to capitalise on the resources they have available. It is essential to any business to use and apply the 'Four Ps' throughout the life cycle of the product, from the 'big idea' stage through the post-sale customer service.

4 Planning and budgeting

No business should be without a 12-month trading plan in the format of a budget. A budget is the best tool a business has to steer its way through periods of uncertainty. It is also beneficial to be able to analyse performance using variance analysis, comparing actual figures with those budgeted. A budget set at the beginning of a fixed period should then be the basis of re-forecasting, which takes in new information that will have an impact on the business plan.

5 Decision making

Management accounting provides the business manager with information upon which informed operational and strategic decisions can be made. There are specific techniques that the management accountant will apply to the data extracted from the company and its business environment. These include decision trees, net present value calculations and variance analysis. This data should be both financial and non-financial and will take into consideration known and assumed factors.

Part 2 Business management and operations

6 Management accounting pack

Business managers should use a management accounting pack (MAP) on a periodic basis to access and track business performance. Items in the pack should include a profit and loss statement, balance sheet, cashflow statement, variance analysis, product and customer profitability analysis and other key ratios that are particularly relevant to the company. A MAP should be bespoke and should provide clear, concise information that is relevant to all parties who wish to use the document.

7 Organisational management

People are expensive and indeed salaries are quite often the biggest expense item for a business. Errors in human resource management can be costly in terms of cashflow, profits and credibility, so it is important to ensure that appropriate methodology is in place to use effectively all the labour hours available within the company.

8 Project management

Not all of the operations of the company will be day-to-day activities. Often there will be a requirement to have a side project to determine a potential outcome of a strategy, or perhaps implementation of a new product or internal function. A project should have a defined strategy from the beginning of the planning phase and those who are involved in its management should be aware of specific techniques that save the company time and money.

9 Information systems

Regardless of the size of a company, information is important to the smooth operations of its internal management and external communication and perception. An information strategy will ensure that the parties who should know relevant data have access to, and make efficient use of, that data. It is often an area of a commercial enterprise that is overlooked by management as they see it as something that should happen naturally. It doesn't – unless an effective strategy is put in place and communicated to the relevant parties.

10 Contract law

Contracts are everywhere and are entered into every day. A small business owner/manager should have at least a basic practical knowledge of the concept of offer and acceptance. Employees, customers, suppliers, directors, shareholders and many other stakeholders of the business will require a contract with the company. A little knowledge can go a long way and prevent problems in the future.

Part 3 Corporate finance

11 Corporate finance for small businesses

Not just the domain of City bankers, owner/managers of SMEs should have a working knowledge of corporate finance options and activities available to them. Corporate finance techniques can save a company relatively large sums of money in terms of cost of capital (debt and equity) and can provide new options for improved working capital and cashflow for current and future projects.

12 Exit

Shareholders of a company will generally have a personal objective regarding an exit from a company in which they hold equity. This objective may not always be in line with the company objective; therefore knowledge of the impact of an exit on the company is integral to any decision regarding the sale of shares. There are also many methods of exit from a company, which should be compared prior to formulation and subsequent execution of an exit strategy.

Business function interactivity

There are many examples of 'business function interactivity' to show how management accounting should encapsulate all business functions to enable fully informed, accurate business decisions to be made (Table 0.1). Once you have accepted this concept, you will understand that an efficient owner/

Table 0.1 Business function interactivity

Issue: Part way through the year, an internal marketing report suggests that market demand has changed and unit sales price should be increased

Business function	Action
Business planning	Unit sales price decided at business planning stage will need to be re-forecasted.
Working capital	Analyse impact of re-forecasted cash flow from sales on working capital forecasts. Surplus cash should be used to maximum advantage.
Marketing	Continue to review market demands and competitor response.
Contract law	Potential obligations to honour original sales price set to customers. An increase may constitute a breach of contract.
Budgeting	Original budget upon which the profit and loss statement is built is now based on non-current information, so the company should re-forecast sales and profitability.
MAP	Monthly reporting updates on performance and the impact on all areas of the business from a unit sales price increase.
Organisational management	Employees should have the skills to support the company through a time of change.
Information systems	Ensure flow of relevant and timely information from marketing to finance and management to provide informational basis for further decisions to be made if required.
Decision making	Management carry out analysis of the change in unit sales price using management accounting tools.
Corporate finance	Options for use of additional working capital should be reviewed, such as dividends or investment.
Exit	Potential impact on valuation of the company and its attractiveness to a buyer.

manager of an SME must incorporate good analysis, planning and control tools into the entire business – this is the concept of management accounting.

Before we move on to look at some management accounting techniques, let's cover some basic administrative issues that a small business will encounter upon start-up and through its corporate life. The administration of the company is also a function that ultimately falls to the owner/manager and it is the director's responsibility to ensure that all administrative and legal considerations are upheld.

What legal form should your small business take?

If you want to run and operate a business, generally a private, limited company is the best vehicle to use. This corporate entity provides the shareholders with financial exposure limited to the value of their shares and is widely recognised as the preferred trading platform for SMEs in the UK. Customers and suppliers will generally expect to trade with a limited company over a private individual and feel comfortable with the level of security that this brings.

Setting up a limited company

Setting up a limited company is incredibly straightforward and can be done without the use of accountants or lawyers. Companies House (www.companies house.org.uk) is a wonderful, free resource for information on how to set up a limited company and meet ongoing administrative obligations.

You will need four documents to set up a limited company. These are:

- Memorandum of Association;
- Articles of Association;
- Form 10;
- Form 12.

The first two of these documents can be gained from any legal stationers for a minimal fee and the latter two, Forms 10 and 12, can be obtained from Companies House directly. Once these forms have been filled out and signed, send them along with a cheque for £20 to Companies House and within 10 days you will have your registered limited company through which to operate.

VAT registration

If your turnover is planned to be more than £61,000 (effective 1 April 2006), it is generally advisable that you register your company for VAT. This means that you should start charging VAT on your invoices if you are providing a taxable service or product. Once registered, your business can claim back VAT on all supplier invoices, where charged. Many businesses that don't register for VAT lose out on not being able to claim back the VAT on their expenses, which leads to lost working capital.

Again, the set-up and administration of VAT is straightforward and needn't involve the use of an accountant or tax expert. Follow the advice of HM Revenue & Customs who are generally contactable and helpful, and ensure that your returns are submitted as required, usually quarterly. Generally it is a small inconvenience for being able to claw back up to 17.5 per cent of your taxable expenditure.

Corporate governance and compliance

Each year, Companies House will require at least two reports from all limited companies in the UK, which are the annual accounts and the annual return. Both are easy to produce and, if you are maintaining up-to-date financial records, should not require any new information to be generated.

Annual accounts

An SME is allowed to submit abbreviated, un-audited accounts to Companies House, which is good news for the business owner as this will save both time and money. Provided your business has maintained good financial records throughout the year, annual accounts can be prepared in a matter of hours. The information sent to the Registrar of Companies at Companies House should include the following:

- profit and loss statement (summary);
- balance sheet (summary);
- audit exemption statements (obtain the wording from Companies House directly);
- directors' statement (brief statement of affairs throughout the year and plan for next year, explaining any significant issues).

The directors of the company will have 10 months after the financial year end to lodge these accounts.

Annual return

The annual return is the government's way of checking on who owns and runs companies within the UK. Each year a pre-printed annual return statement will be sent to the company secretary from Companies House, to which you should make any changes to shareholder or director information.

Compliance and corporate governance for a small business should cost very little in terms of management time and company money. When in doubt seek advice from the appropriate agency.

What exactly is an SME?

Basically, a 'small to medium-sized enterprise' must meet two of the three criteria as set out below:

	Small	**Medium**
Turnover	£5.6m	£22.8m
Balance sheet balance	£2.8m	£11.4m
Average number of employees	50	250

If you have an SME, you are part of a special group of companies that are integral to the UK economy and the wider business environment. Treat your SME as the directors of the FTSE 250 treat their companies and ensure that you maximise your profits through taking full advantage of the resources available to your business. The application of management accounting techniques can help you do this without introducing unnecessary bureaucracy and administration.

Good luck!

1

Business planning and analysis

Business planning

One of the most important tasks an SME owner/manager will ever perform, when launching a company or project, is to write a business plan. Without a well thought out and researched business plan, a business may not reach its full potential or even make it off the starting block. With a good idea and a great business plan there should be no stopping a motivated individual from setting up and managing a successful SME.

A business plan must be many things to many people, but above all it will be well thought out and must contain a great deal of information while being concise. If you get it right, it could be your ticket to funding for further growth and development of your company.

Why use a business plan?

Business plans are used for many reasons, depending on the nature of the entrepreneurial idea, strategy and the objectives involved in starting, developing, growing or exiting a company.

Reasons for developing a business plan include:

- Budget for financial planning and analysis.
- Raise finance.
- Attract investment in terms of money or an individual's time (mentor).
- Improve performance of an existing business.
- Appeal to suppliers.

- Attract customers.
- Entice key employees to join the team.

A business plan will set out what you wish to achieve in terms of objectives and how you intend to achieve these objectives.

The relevance of management accounting to effective business planning

Management accounting approaches business planning from an all-encompassing perspective. It is integral to look at the whole of the business, its immediate internal environment and the external environment such as economic and regulatory issues that may impact on the company.

It is not enough to enter some figures into a spreadsheet, whip up a graph or two and write some blurb about your product and how great it is. A business plan must display your working knowledge of all aspects of the environment in which you plan to operate the company.

Management accounting techniques that enable this analysis include:

- The competitive environment through the Stakeholder Interactivity Model (covered in detail later in this chapter).
- SWOT analysis – analysing the strengths, weaknesses, opportunities and threats of the business (covered in Chapter 4).
- Variance analysis – this shows for the difference between the actual outcome of the business activity, such as sales, against the planned performance of the business (covered in Chapter 5).
- Application of accounting principles to ensure that the financial section of the business plan is robust and will hold when applied in practice. The four basic accounting fundamentals are: prudence, consistency, matching and going concern. These basic accounting terms are explained in the glossary section of this book.
- Marketing analysis – consider the 'Four Ps' of marketing, which are price, placement, product and promotion (covered in Chapter 3).

There are many management accounting techniques which will play a role in one or more sections of your business plan. These will be covered in more detail later in the book; however, for now, let's consider what is needed for the actual business plan document.

What makes a good business plan?

A business plan must cover every aspect of your company. Use this useful reminder of what is critical in a good business plan:

B Businesslike – professionalism is critical in appealing to a potential investor or stakeholder. Your business plan is likely to be the first exposure to your project, so ensure that you make a positive impression by presenting your plan in a proficient manner in keeping with your proposed audience.

U Understandable – while you may understand the intricacies of your business, it is unlikely that others would; therefore ensure that the language you use can be understood by a layperson, ie someone who is not from the industry or trade. Ensure that complex ideas and language are made clear to ensure that your message is being understood.

S Simple – an overriding principle in all aspects of business is to keep things simple. You should not overcomplicate your company's concept by trying to say or do too much. If in doubt, leave it out – yes, it's a cliché, but it also happens to make good practical sense in this case.

I Interesting – keep the reader's attention with statistics and data that will support your argument. An all-text document can be difficult to keep interesting, so break it up with graphs and charts to support your points.

N New – it is likely that the person reading your business plan will be given hundreds of 'money-making schemes' and 'the latest big thing' concepts in a month. Make yours stand out by ensuring that you have something new and exciting to capture the interest and imagination of the reader.

E Exceptional – your company must offer the investor something that he or she cannot get from another source. You and your business proposal must be unique and should provide a unique product or service or an individual angle on an existing product or service.

S Supported – your commercial and financial claims must be supported or be able to be backed up if asked. For example, if you say your idea is likely to attract 5 per cent of a £200m market, you must be able to provide a basis for your calculation on the 5 per cent and statistical references to the £200m. This will be asked of you at some point, so do not make a claim that cannot be supported, as it will cause all of your figures to be called into question.

S Succinct – the document should be jargon free and to the point. Don't waffle on any point. The idea that someone who knows what he or she is talking about says fewer words rings true, so keep it short and snappy.

P Positive – while being realistic, you should be positive when displaying your concepts and how your ideas will transform into a profitable business. Don't forget that a common purpose of the business plan is to sell something to someone.

L Length – I was once told by a financier that if a business plan is more than 10 pages long, he won't even turn the first page. It's so hard to know the right length and often there isn't one. Use the general rule of thumb of around 10 pages on an initial business plan and offer additional information if the reader cares to enquire further about a specific section of the plan.

A Accurate – all information must be accurate and, once written, tested for its integrity before the business plan is released. If one figure is erroneous, the whole of your argument will be called into question.

N Numbers – the most important point is kept for last. It doesn't matter how unique, exciting or desirable your business concept is, if it doesn't make sense financially it won't attract investment. Ensure that your numbers are well presented, accurate and give the potential investor or stakeholder the ability to earn a return on their investment.

Writing the business plan

Think about what you want to achieve with your business plan. This will give you an idea of the areas on which to focus and how to display certain information.

A beneficial activity to carry out before actually writing the document, which can be an onerous task, is to brainstorm the information that will be covered in later chapters of this book as a guide. Brainstorming at this early stage is useful in order to cover as many aspects of the new business as possible. Start with a large clean sheet of paper and write down any idea, concept, concern, issue – both positive and negative – that you can think of about the new enterprise. Keep referring back to this initial brainstorm as it is easy to lose sight of the things that were important at the beginning once the operation starts.

Information and analysis gained from the data entered into the management accounting models will add necessary and relevant detail to the following recommended sections of the business plan.

The following structure should be used as your guide when using your raw data, research and ideas to create a business plan. Each business is different and therefore each business plan should take on its own identity; however, it should cover specific basic information.

Structure of a typical business plan

Your business plan should have three main sections:

1. commercial – which tells the reader about the business and its purpose;
2. financial – how the company will make money;
3. appendices – supporting documents referred to in the main body.

In addition, you should have a title page, table of contents and an introduction page which will act as a summary of the business plan.

Let's look at each of these main sections in more detail.

Commercial

- The purpose and overall objectives of the business should be outlined by stating what you are trying to achieve in terms of the product, the market and financials.
- Provide details of the product. What is its unique selling point, advantages and any other issues surrounding the product?
- The key individuals who are important to the company should be outlined, each with a short biography addressing relevant education, experience and what they contribute to the business.
- Marketing is crucial for business success, so provide a plan of the pricing, placement (where you will sell the product), customers and competitors (covered in Chapter 3).

Financial

- Profit and loss statement – shows the level of turnover, gross profit, overheads and net profit for the company. This should be detailed for year 1 and summarised quarterly for years 2 to 3.
- Balance sheet – provides a snapshot of the assets and liabilities of the company at any given time, which should provide an opening and closing position each year for three years.
- Cashflow statement – the opening balance, cash movement in a period and closing cash balance should be provided monthly for year 1 and summarised quarterly for years 2 to 3.

- Basis of company valuation – a brief statement on how you are valuing the business proposal; for example, are you using a percentage of turnover or multiples of profit? There are many ways of valuing a company which will be looked at in more detail in the corporate finance part of this book.
- Required investment and proposal – how much money do you need and what are you prepared to offer, in return for the funding? Consider if you will also benefit from a mentor, so a component of this requirement might be time from a proven business professional who could perhaps enhance your company's performance and image.

Appendices

- financial reports;
- relevant photographs or images;
- price lists;
- press releases or advertisements.

Each of the above points will be reviewed in greater length throughout the book. An entrepreneur should be able to write a good, solid business plan to appeal to a wide range of audiences and this skill will become second nature; however, first it must be learnt!

How to get started writing your business plan

When setting out a business plan, it is useful to brainstorm details and data from a wide range of areas within the company. The Stakeholder Interactivity Model is a useful guide for this initial planning as it helps the planner to consider the internal and external environment of the company.

The Stakeholder Interactivity Model (Figure 1.1) takes into consideration the main stakeholders that will make up the integral relationships that will shape your company. First, who are your stakeholders?

Stakeholders

There are internal and external parties who will play a role in helping, and sometimes hindering, your business on its path to success. People and

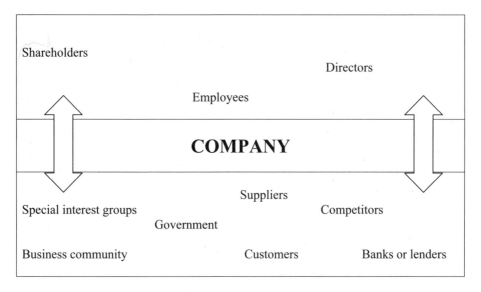

INTERNAL

Shareholders

Directors

Employees

COMPANY

Suppliers

Special interest groups   Competitors

Government

Business community   Customers   Banks or lenders

EXTERNAL

Figure 1.1   Stakeholder Interactivity Model

businesses that have a direct relationship with your company are called stakeholders. It is worth knowing who they are and how you can maximise the potential out of your relationship with them.

Banks

Your relationship with your bank can be a critical one in both the set-up and operational phases of a business. Once they have bought into your business plan, they may offer to extend you some working capital. Working capital is money or other liquid asset that can be called upon quickly to fund the operations of the business. The bank's objective is to receive capital and interest repayments on the due date. There are common goals between the parties in that the bank wants to see your business succeed so that you can continue to make these repayments. Often they will lend money linked to some security and therefore your objective is also to safeguard that asset. Security will either be a company asset or, where these are not of sufficient value, personal assets of one or more of the directors.

Competitors

Competitors can be a great source of information. Look where they have succeeded and failed before and learn from their lessons. It can also be useful to enter a market where the consumer has already been educated on a similar product offering as this can be a costly marketing activity.

Customers (debtors)

Customer relationships can be difficult to manage. Without them you don't have a business and yet they will undoubtedly test your patience over the start-up phase and far beyond! The old adage 'the customer is always right' should be at the forefront of your mind and, where possible, bend and stretch your way around their needs; however, keep them under control. You are their creditor and as such they may try to extend credit terms to improve their cashflow. Most companies do this, so you must keep credit control tight, while maintaining a positive relationship with your customers.

Directors

If this is your company, you will probably be a director. It is likely that you will have at least one other director, whether or not you choose this individual. It may be someone you have chosen because of their business acumen or a complementary characteristic, or perhaps your investor requires a board seat as a condition of funding. Either way, the directors are collectively responsible for the corporate governance of the company and should be able to represent the business in its best possible light.

Employees

Employees will be looking to your business to advance their own careers and maximise their rewards by way of salary, experience and other benefits. They will weigh up the benefit of working for you against working for an alternative employer and will go for the most self-serving option. There are exceptions, of course, but generally this is how employees approach deciding who they work for. Through promoting goal congruence, you can get the best out of your employees while getting the best for you and your business. Set common goals and monitor them to ensure that the employee is working to best serve the company's objectives. The organisational management of the company is covered in Chapter 7.

Government

The government can be both a great ally and a hindrance to your enterprise. Their objectives are politically motivated and will rarely be flexible around your specific business requirements. It is worth investigating the benefits to small business on offer from the government, such as start-up information and support packs, grants, and training initiatives for employees. While the government often does its best to help small business, they equally must ensure that legislation is being followed and this is where the burden of bureaucracy can be an obstacle to small business. Issues such as taxation, health and safety legislation and employee records can be time consuming and often confusing.

Neighbours and your local business community

Look around you. Are you in a business park or in an area where there are other businesses large or small? If so, there are probably benefits and cost savings that can be gained from your environment. Joining up with other companies can provide an SME with economies of scale normally enjoyed only by larger companies.

Shareholders

Maximising wealth is the main aim of shareholders. They take the risk and therefore should reap the rewards. Some shareholders may have provided assets in return for shares, so the director's duty is also to protect their assets. Most investors, such as investment companies and business angels (high net worth individuals), will have some input other than just cash, such as contacts and expertise, the potential of which you should maximise. Sometimes investors wish to be silent, retaining an element of anonymity, which should also be respected. The greater the shareholding of a shareholder, the greater his or her influence and power over the business will be, so take this into consideration when distributing equity. While it's important to raise money if required, it is also very important to be able to have a positive working relationship with these very important stakeholders.

Special interest groups

Think about groups who may relate to your product or market. Are there any groups that can help promote or spread the word about your business? A popular technique used by start-ups, who have limited capital for marketing, is to use 'advertorials'. Advertorials feature as special interest pieces in the media to provide information and commentary on a new product or personality. Find special interest groups by searching the internet and asking people who already work in the sector. Make these groups and their networks work for you.

Suppliers (creditors)

Your creditors are likely to be companies with their own profit motive and will have the objective of wanting timely payment in line with agreed payment terms. Your company is likely to want to extend payment terms as much as possible to retain precious cash reserves, and so the tug of war begins.

It is important to find a stakeholder–management balance that works for your company. How you approach your stakeholder relationships and maximise the benefits that can be gained from each group can make a very real impact on the success of your company.

Timescale of the business plan

Allow around three months to write your business plan, which includes time to do some thorough market and product research. By the time you come to actually write your plan, you should have sufficient notes on each section of the outline mentioned earlier in this chapter. Use this as a guide when collecting relevant information to ensure you're ready to compile and write the finished document.

Sometimes you may not have the luxury of time to complete a full business plan. It is the first document a potential investor will want to see and you may have to work to their timescales.

Enforced timescales

I have been asked at 8:45am to build a business plan within one working day to be submitted by 5pm that evening. In this particular instance, my client was looking for funding from a company that had their board meeting the following day and had to have his business plan in time otherwise it would not be considered for another six months. I had to prioritise as I had no time to put together a fully researched and presented business plan. I asked the potential investor what was the key information he was looking for, as he understood the time constraints. The answer was profitability, so I focused on providing a profitability schedule with supporting documents. The submission was a success and my client received an investment proposal from the company less than a month later.

Review the final document

Once you have completed your business plan, leave it to one side for a couple of days, then go back and read it again. A fresh mind may see errors in the text or presentation or perhaps improvements that can be made to the overall content.

It is also a good idea to ask an individual whom you trust to review the document and provide feedback. Choose two people – someone who has little knowledge and someone who knows some detail of your business concept to ensure that you have used the correct level of language and terminology to suit a range of potential readers.

When you're happy with the final document, it is important for it to look professional, so I would recommend having it printed in colour and bound by a professional. There are many high-street printers and stationers who can do this for you cost-effectively.

What to do with your completed business plan

How do you know to whom you should send your business plan? Go back to what you are trying to achieve by compiling the business plan in the first place. Establish who your readers will be, discover full contact details (especially the full name of the individual whom you wish to read the business plan) and prepare a pack of information to send to them. This pack should include a covering letter, the business plan and a stamped, self-addressed envelope if you wish feedback or even the business plan to be returned to you.

It is best to make an introductory call or have a third-party introduction to the desired recipient of your business plan. This will ensure that you are sending it to the right person and will prepare them for receipt of the information rather than have it appear as unsolicited mail.

Potential recipients of your business plan may include:

- funding – bank manager, business angels, corporate financiers, investment banks;
- supplier contracts – your preferred supplier list;
- key staff – it often takes a leap of faith for an individual to join a start-up operation, so an effective business plan might alleviate any nervousness about leaving a stable job to join a new or developing company.

Once you have sent the pack off, you will hopefully be given an opportunity to follow this up with a personal presentation of the business plan. Use this time to prepare your presentation – know your figures immediately and accurately. You should be able to 'present' the contents of your business plan confidently without notes – not necessarily verbatim, but certainly intimate knowledge of the facts and figures is essential.

Is there an alternative to a business plan?

Business planning is critical to the success of a business and it is not recommended that any short-cuts or alternatives to a business plan be applied. Gone are the days of a 'business plan' scribbled on the back of an envelope that obtains millions of pounds in funding. Thankfully, those heady days of internet and concept companies are behind us and we now operate in an environment where strong, well-developed and well-managed businesses come out on top.

Having said that, not all business plans need to fit into the same mould, as all businesses are different. Some businesses may be able to start trading and gain working capital or financing based on a brief financial overview of the company, whereas others will require a 20-page document that analyses all possible risks and rewards of an investor entering into the business.

Look at business planning as an exercise that will improve the efficiency of the business, not just as a tool to gain entry to a market or win financing. A business plan will always be worth the time and energy put into it at some point in the life of the company.

Case studies

The director of Telecoms Co developed a business plan primarily to use as a pricing model for the service, which the company was to provide. He knew the operating profit he wanted to achieve and the cost price, so he developed a model that would give him an optimal sales price. The director remembers the importance of having a concise business plan to present to external parties. 'It all grew from there. Once we had that model in place, the rest of the business plan was built around it. It was essential that we had a formal business plan as we were looking for some kind of external funding or partnership and having a clear, concise plan of our activities enabled us to obtain that.' On the strength of the business plan alone, Telecoms Co secured several agreements with major international telecommunication providers, which has proven to be highly beneficial to the company's success.

Bath Co developed their business plan for a new product from scratch as they had previously traded without a formal plan, until such point as they realised they needed to have tighter controls on the business. Their business plan focused on the main commercial constraint, which was cash, so the cashflow statement was the centre of the business plan. Based on the strength of the newly created plan, they were able to secure interim external financing, which enabled the company to grow in line with their forecasts.

Conclusion

The importance of having a business plan should not be underestimated, which is why it is Chapter 1 of this book. Management accounting techniques can be used to build a strong, thorough and concise business plan which considers its entire environment and looks at past, present and future events to provide a comprehensive view on the company and its operating environment.

Key points to remember

- Ensure your business plan covers the following key components:

  B Businesslike
  U Understandable
  S Simple
  I Interesting
  N New
  E Exceptional
  S Supported
  S Succinct
  P Positive
  L Length
  A Accurate
  N Numbers

- The guide for the structure of your business plan is:
  - **Commercial**
    - business purpose;
    - product or service information;
    - key people;
    - marketing (price, placement, product, promotion);
    - overall objectives;
  - **Financial**
    - profit and loss statement;
    - balance sheet;
    - cashflow statement;
    - basis of company valuation;
    - required investment and proposal;
  - **Appendices**
    - financial schedules;
    - relevant photographs or images;
    - price lists;
    - press releases or advertisements.
- Work to timescale set by others effectively – prioritise information.
- Present the document professionally.
- Send the business plan out to identified individuals and organisations.
- Practise presenting your business plan.

2

Working capital management

An important part of running a successful SME is working capital management. Working capital is the assets and liabilities of a company that are sufficiently liquid so that the company can 'work' them as part of day-to-day activities. The term 'liquid' in this sense means assets that can be spent, used or traded immediately or with short notice.

In terms of your balance sheet, working capital is stated as:

Current assets – Current liabilities = Working capital

Working capital is also a measure of solvency of a company as it indicates that a business can pay its current debt with its current assets.

The 'correct' amount of working capital employed largely depends on the industry, the financial structure and the life of the company and its annual sales cycle. The key is to ensure that there is sufficient working capital to pay debts as and when they fall due.

The relevance of management accounting to working capital management

Management accounting techniques can be applied to monitor the controls of current assets and current liabilities, the most important of which is cash. From the start-up phase through to management of a mature business, working capital management is an important part of running the business, so ensure that you have the appropriate tools in place to monitor the company's liquidity levels.

Cash is king

Cash is without question the most important resource in your business. The treatment of cash, from initial development through to operating and selling your company, will be the difference between success and failure and you rarely get a second chance to right wrongs.

Profits do not equal cash

Cash is all about the timing of cash inflows and outflows. When focusing on your liquidity, forget about accounting issues such as accruals and profits – just consider what cash items are actually coming in and going out of the business. Also, don't forget about discounts that may have been promised, which your customers can deduct from their payment to the company.

Case study

The directors of a client of mine, who produce and sell wholesale luxury items, created a healthy profit and loss budget, which was detailed in terms of product margin and overall profitability for the business. They forecast a good profit for the year, which to them automatically translated to a cash surplus. When I forecast out the cash movement for the year and reported that they would have a deficit, they did not understand how they could be making profits and still be relying on an expensive overdraft to fund their working capital.

One of the directors came to me saying she had spent sleepless nights over this issue for weeks and just couldn't understand how this could be the case. My response was – profits do not equal cash. Profits are an accounting statement, certainly a good sign that the business is doing well, but it won't always correspond to a cash surplus that matches the profit.

I explained to the director that the key is to think logically about cash – it reflects the exact timing requirements of cash. If something is due in August, it is paid in August. Accounting isn't as logical as it's all to do with the 'matching' accounting principle. If a sale is recognised in June, then the associated costs should also be stated in the June profit and loss statement – even if the actual cash goes out in August.

It's a very important distinction to make, as I have seen many companies use the profit and loss statement to manage their cashflow and have found that their figures very rarely add up.

Some of the key reasons for the timing difference include:

- debtor and credit repayment agreements;
- stock purchases and lead-time;
- accruals and prepayments;
- depreciation of fixed assets.

Have a think about how closely your profit and loss statement relates to the actual cash movement in your business. If it's largely a cash business with fast-moving stock then you will probably find that your profit and loss statement is a good reflection of cashflow; however, once the above-mentioned items start creeping in, you could see the two diverge.

Even if you are making profits, if you don't have the cash to pay debts as and when they fall due, your company could be put into liquidation or have some operational constraints imposed by a creditor.

Cashflow forecasts

Keep daily cash forecasts in the early days, forecasting 12 weeks in detail and then in summary for a fixed, rolling period after that. Generally, the planning horizon on a cashflow forecast is longer than that of a profit and loss statement. The application of a planning horizon is explained in more detail in Chapter 4.

When you know your business well enough – after at least 12 months – weekly forecasts should provide sufficient controls. Keep this separate from your other forecasts as this will be your most important control tool. Monitor variance analysis tightly and analyse any significant movements or variances – both positive and adverse. Variance analysis is analysing the difference between actual and planned performance, as is explained in more detail in Chapter 5 on decision making.

Case study

The wholesale telecoms market has always been a volatile one, so with this in mind the director of Telecoms Co decided to keep an eye on his cashflow daily. This soon paid off as he picked up a large accounting error from one of his suppliers, which could have crippled his business if it had not been identified earlier. A supplier was paying on a different pricing rate than that agreed. Reconciliation at point of invoice would have meant that Telecoms Co would have been two weeks behind in the working capital cycle as disputed invoices tend to take longer to pay. He knew the cash he expected to receive on a daily basis and when it was different, he knew immediately that there was a problem. Thanks to the cashflow forecast, this was a small blip in the process rather than a potentially fatal situation for his fledgling start-up.

Cash deficit

If you are looking at a cash deficit in your forecast, take immediate steps to ensure it doesn't adversely impact on operations. This may require a call to the bank manager to discuss a short-term overdraft, extending terms with suppliers or calling upon directors for loans. Focus on the core business through difficult cash-poor times, as this is no time for non-essential spend.

Case study

Ad Co, an advertising agency, was faced with being closed down by its parent company. The directors agreed to the advice given, which was to cut out non-essential spend until such time as the company was making money and could make the parent company feel secure that it was a viable trading entity. The directive went out to staff that all non-essential spend was to cease, effective immediately, the alternative being that the workforce would have to be cut to save money. Some of the cost savings that were made were non-essential expenses for staff such as gym memberships, bowls of fruit and bottled drinks, entertainment and travel. Despite the seriousness of the situation, employees were screaming for their M&S apples and their cans of coke, despite the threat of losing their jobs. Look at the big picture. It may require your staff to come on board and understand the nature of the constraint.

Contingency

There will always be an item of expenditure that unexpectedly pops up at a time when the company is running on limited cashflow. The best forecasts cannot plan for every eventuality, so it is essential to have some form of contingency planning in place. I generally allow for 2 per cent of turnover per month as cash contingency.

Remember – cash is king and cash does not necessarily equal profits. Forecast and keep a firm eye on the flow of cash against the business forecast, and you will be a step ahead of the game.

Methods of cashflow management

Cashflow can be improved by reducing stocks and debtors, adopting more credit or perhaps taking a bridging loan. Let's look at each of these methods of cashflow management in turn, before looking at working capital management analysis techniques.

Stockholding

High stock levels can be an expensive luxury for a lean business as this ties up capital and adds to the cost of stockholding.

If your business has, or is intending to hold stock, it is imperative that you plan the most effective method of holding and accounting for stock. The reason for this is that the working capital must be financed somehow, through either debt or equity, and both are costs to the business. Holding on to extra stock not only increases the costs of financing the working capital needed, but also increases the actual cost of stockholding (eg warehousing), as well as an increased risk that the stock may become obsolete and will not be able to be sold or may have to be sold at a discount. The idea behind an efficient stockholding method is to keep stock levels and the associated costs to the business at an absolute minimum while being able to supply demand as it occurs.

The balance is an extremely difficult one to get right and many companies struggle to calculate their optimal amount of stock. Issues that may upset the balance are:

- changing customer demands;
- changing seasonality (no rain in April for an umbrella producer);
- competitor influences, such as lower pricing or new product;
- supply of raw materials from supplier;
- problems with the manufacturer;
- warehousing and delivery issues, such as insufficient labour to fulfil orders when required;
- lost or stolen stock or finished goods.

The list could go on and on. Think about factors that are relevant to your business, the market and industry in which you operate. I find it useful to draw a diagram of the whole process (similar to our cash operating cycle featured in the section later in this chapter) and think about what could go wrong in the cycle. Try to plan for what you know and make an educated guess on what could happen. There is no method that will ensure that every eventuality is planned for; however, you should be able to plan sufficiently to ensure that you find a balance between stockholding and supplying customer demand when required.

Stockholding methods

There are many stockholding methods that management accountants apply to business operations and analysis. There are three methods that have been tried and tested on the SME market and work well to provide an efficient stockholding balance. There is no correct method out of these three; however, one of them will be best suited to your business and it is this method that should be applied. Don't try to use two methods together as this has been proven to fail. Choose the method that best suits your business model.

Just in time (JIT)

The basis of JIT stockholding is that raw materials arrive just in time for production into the work in progress (WIP) cycle and then the finished good is ready just in time for distribution to the market, where there is a ready demand for the product. This is a very difficult process to perfect, though it is the optimal approach to stockholding.

Last in first out (LIFO)

The last item of finished good is the first to be sent out for sale. This is easy to monitor; however, it risks the first becoming obsolete or damaged by remaining in stock for too long. There are some products where LIFO works well, such as fast-moving, consistent, non-perishable items.

First in first out (FIFO)

The FIFO method of stockholding ensures that the oldest stock items are the first to be distributed to the market, which minimises the risk of wastage. This is the preferred method for perishable items or goods that change rapidly with market demands.

Once an appropriate stock method has been established for your company, an economic order quantity (EOQ) formula should be calculated. The EOQ is designed to find the right balance of stockholding whereby costs associated with holding on to stock are minimised.

The EOQ formula is as follows:

$$EOQ = \sqrt{\frac{(2 \times D \times O)}{C}}$$

where:

EOQ = optimum stockholding quantity
D   = annual demand per period
O   = cost of placing an order
C   = cost of carrying a unit of stock per period.

For example, if Cars Ltd sells 20,000 cars per year, placing an order for cars costs £1,000 and the cost of keeping each car in stock is £750, the EOQ would read:

$$EOQ = \sqrt{\frac{(2 \times 20,000 \times £1,000)}{£750}}$$

The EOQ for Cars Ltd would be 231 cars per order.

By placing an order based on the EOQ formula, a company will maximise efficiency in terms of its stock-based working capital.

Debtors and credit control

Companies approach the issue of credit control in different ways. It largely depends on your relationship with your customers, how many there are, and the amounts and terms of their credit, especially in relation to your turnover. The higher the exposure the more attention they should receive from the person controlling cash in your business. Different techniques such as developing a relationship, sending demand letters and even threatening legal action can work wonders – or not at all – which is why it's important to tailor credit control to your business and that of your customer.

Case studies

The director in charge of sales at Telecoms Co is also in charge of cash (debtor) collection. He uses his positive relationships generated with his contacts and is always first on the pay list. When wooing customers, don't forget about the individual who actually makes the payments as they have a lot of control over when you get paid. Quite often the senior management sign whichever cheques are put in front of them and it is the junior in Accounts who makes up the pay list. This is a point considered by Telecoms Co and the director never fails to say hello to the accounts team when he's meeting with senior management.

An alternative and quite often preferred collection method, where possible, is cash upfront. Bed Co insists that cash is paid before the goods are delivered, which ensures that they never have a problem with bad debt. They also require a 50 per cent deposit before they order raw materials required for a customer order as their beds are often bespoke pieces, which may not be saleable to another customer. It is, therefore, very important to their business that a customer commits to the purchase.

This method of cash collection also creates much less burden on the working capital cycle as their business does not need to finance work in progress.

Customer vetting

Customer vetting can be a very effective way to prevent bad debt from customers. Prepare a brief and easy-to-use document (no more than one page) to obtain basic information on the customer such as name, address, time spent at address, credit references and credit limit required. This principle can apply to business customers or individuals.

Carrying out customer vetting is a common occurrence in today's business environment and customers will rarely feel that their rights are being violated by being asked to provide basic financial information. They are, however, entitled to refuse to provide this information, in which case they may be perceived as a high-risk creditor.

Contracts

Where possible, ask the customer to agree to and sign a contract for services. A contract is designed to limit the financial and operational exposure of the company, while enabling a remedy (course of legal action) against any customer who refuses to pay for a product or service provided. Make sure the terms of settlement are clear and are written down clearly, agreed and signed by all relevant, authorised parties. There is more information on how to approach the issue of commercial contracts in Chapter 10 on contract law.

Suppliers and purchasing

Using suppliers who are also creditors can be a cheap source of finance. Take credit facilities where given and ensure that you know what discounts are available if you pay on time or even early. These may be stated in the small print of the contract, so read them carefully. Bear in mind that paying early to gain a discount of £100 could mean that you don't have funds for an activity that may net the company £200, so think about the need for working capital for the company before committing funds.

Loan – debt financing

Not all working capital can be generated through profitable business activity. Most companies, at some stage in their lives, will need to secure some form of debt with which to trade. For some, it is a short-term bridging need to see the company through a difficult cash operating cycle, whereas other companies choose debt as a long-term strategic option.

When considering the type of debt required, the following questions should be asked:

- How averse are the owners and directors of the company to debt? If the owners and directors of the company are nervous about gearing the company too highly, it may be that using debt to cover working capital requirements may not be an option. It is possible that an SME will have insufficient assets to act as security for a debt and directors of the company are commonly expected to give personal guarantees on loan amounts.
- How much debt is required and for how long? If the debt is required for only a short amount of time, such as a bridging facility, an overdraft facility may be the easiest option. If the debt is required for a longer period, a lender may need to see business plans, specifically cashflow forecasts, to ensure that the business will be able to pay off the loan in the future.

- How will the company pay the interest and the capital payments? Regardless of who provides the debt financing and what form it takes, a lender will want to understand how a company intends to repay the loan. Internally, the management of the company must ensure that sufficient post-tax profits will be made to finance the debt. Also, ensure that profits made from the increased working capital provided by the debt injection is greater than the cost of the debt itself.
- What are the assets of the company? The lender may require security against a loan, which will require the use of an asset as security. A full and updated list of the assets of the company along with their cost and net book values should be available.
- Can the company take on the amount of debt required and stay solvent? If the loan amount is added to the current liabilities, would this bring the company into an insolvent position? The simple ratio of current assets over current liabilities will provide this answer. If the ratio is one or greater the company remains solvent, if it is less than one, the loan will push the company into an insolvent position. This is not a position of strength for the company and should be considered carefully.

Debt can be a useful tool for both a growing and a mature business. It can also be a noose around a company's neck and can be a major reason for failure if not managed effectively. Working capital management should include management of debt as a priority as it is a cost and a liability to the business.

Invoice factoring

Another method to free up cash in the business is invoice factoring. This is a process whereby a company makes a sale, raises a sales invoice on credit to a customer and then 'sells' that invoice to an invoice factoring company. These companies buy debt. An invoice factoring company will pay the company around 80–90 per cent of the invoice total. The invoice total is not paid in full as the factoring company will provide cash up front, so they need to pay for their own working capital. They will also factor in a percentage for potential bad debt of your customers, thereby offering a reduced invoice total.

Invoice factoring can work in some situations and it can be an effective way to improve a working capital cycle. However, most invoice factoring companies will require some security over bad debts in addition to control over your debtors (who are also your customers). This perception is not always positive as companies who use invoice factoring often do so because their financial performance is not strong. Also, the factoring company may also want to control the bank account of the company or require a new bank account to be set up with one of their directors as co-signatory on all outgoings.

It is a method that can work, though it would be wise to consider all other options before introducing invoice factoring to your business.

The cash operating cycle

In terms of working capital management, it is important to monitor how many days the cash asset of the business is held through the cash operating cycle. The aim is to keep the days in the cycle to a minimum and compare the number of days against previous months to ensure that control and efficiency are achieved and maintained.

Note that the theory of the cash operating cycle is based on credit sales, rather than pro forma, or up-front, cash payment (Figure 2.1).

There are five stages to the cash operating cycle, each of which should be managed both independently and as part of the overall process. The five stages are:

1. Raw materials or components purchased. The company pays its suppliers for raw materials or stock for production. At this point, cash leaves the company and is passed to the supplier from whom the materials have been purchased. The cash enters the cycle and should be calculated in terms of 'days held in raw materials'.
2. Stock used to produce goods – work in progress (WIP). Once the raw materials have been received from the supplier, they enter the processing of creating finished goods. This process is called work in progress and can be a matter of days or months depending on the product type and the complexity of its manufacture. Cash remains tied up in the cycle and is calculated as 'days held in WIP'.
3. Finished goods are ready for distribution. The WIP function has turned the raw materials into finished goods, which are ready to be distributed to retailers (or wholesalers). The company still has not yet received any cash for these items, so further days in the cycle should be termed 'days in pending retail'.

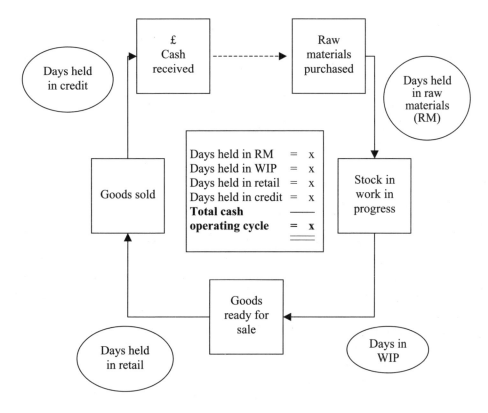

Figure 2.1   Cash operating cycle

4. Goods are held by retailers and sold. The goods are now ready for sale by the retailer (or wholesaler). Upon sale to the customer, the retailer receives their payment for the goods which will be the company's payment plus the retailer's commission or mark-up. Cash is nearing the end of its cycle and days in this part of the cycle are termed 'days held in credit' as the company has effectively provided the retailer with credit owing to a time delay between the collected customer payment for the goods and the transfer of the money to the company.
5. Cash received to the company. The end of the cash operating cycles sees the company receiving the money from the sale of the goods purchased as raw materials at the beginning of the cycle.

Once the entire cycle has been analysed and the number of days in each part of the cycle have been added together, the company can establish the total number of days it does not have use of this liquid current asset. The aim is to reduce this number of days without having an adverse impact on the efficiency of the production cycle.

Compare the number of days with the previous month to establish a pattern of where large delays of cash holding occur in the business. For example, an umbrella company may have a long cash operating cycle during the months leading up to the rainy season. This can be identified and appropriately planned for by understanding the cash operating cycle of their business.

Ratio analysis

Before looking at ratios, let's remind ourselves of the component parts of the financial structure of the company that makes up working capital, as it is these accounting areas that will be used to calculate the ratios. Working capital is current assets minus current liabilities. A balance sheet will refer to working capital as net current assets.

Working capital measures the value of liquid assets a company has available with which to build its business. In general, companies who have a lot of working capital should be more successful since they can expand and improve their operations. Companies with a cash deficit may lack the funds necessary for growth.

Management accounting relies on ratios to calculate and monitor working capital statistics that help manage an SME.

Once calculated, set up these ratios as part of a monthly reporting document (such as the management accounting pack as detailed in Chapter 6). It is important to ensure that each time these ratios are calculated, the same source data and methodology are applied to ensure consistency. This consistency of data collection will provide integrity of information required for comparability from one period to the next, which will help a manager make good business decisions.

Solvency

Current assets : Current liabilities

If total current assets is greater than total current liabilities, then the company is solvent. If not, the company is in an insolvent position and should consider the future as to why it remains a going concern.

Acid test ratio

(Current assets – stock) : Total current liabilities

The acid test ratio is the clearest measure of how well the company is covering its short-term obligations, since the ratio only considers that part of current assets which can be turned into cash immediately (thus the exclusion of stock). It's called the acid test ratio as it tells stakeholders how much of a company's debt it could cover if the company was liquidated quickly.

The ratio will provide a number – the higher the number, the healthier the company. This ratio is seen as a sign of a company's strength or weakness and should be carried out as part of the monthly financial analysis. It is certainly a statistic that will be used by external parties when considering your company as a creditor or even debtor. The fact that this ratio is so widely used is another good reason to keep stockholding to a minimum (as covered in the stockholding section earlier in this chapter).

Cash asset ratio (liquidity ratio)

Total value of cash assets : Total current liabilities

The cash asset ratio measures the extent to which a company can quickly liquidate assets and cover short-term liabilities. It is therefore of interest to short-term creditors to ensure that their debts can be paid.

Conclusion

Working capital is a fundamental part of a successful business. The effective management of the cash, debtors, creditors, loan debt and other current assets and liabilities will provide the working capital a business needs to be resilient and to grow.

Working capital should be managed with a strategy tailor-made for a company by the application of management accounting tools presented in this chapter. This analysis will become the cornerstone of the financial management of the company.

Key points to remember

Working capital is defined as:

- Current assets – Current liabilities = Working capital (refer to your balance sheet for these figures).
- Working capital is a measure of solvency of a company. Solvency is a company's ability to pay its debts as and when they fall due.
- Cash is king – cash is the most important resource in a start-up or SME.
- Profits do not equal cash – cash is about timings of inflows and outflows of cash, not necessarily profit or loss.
- Generate cashflow forecasts in detail for a period of 12 weeks and in summary for at least 12 months.
- Methods of cashflow management include:
  - stockholding:
    - just in time (JIT);
    - last in first out (LIFO);
    - first in first out (FIFO);
    - (an economic order quantity (EOQ) is useful to calculate optimal stockholding levels);
  - debtors and credit control;
  - customer vetting;
  - contracts;
  - suppliers and purchasing;
  - loan – debt financing;
  - invoice factoring.
- Cash operating cycle. Follow the five stages of cash movement around the operations of the business to ensure its most efficient use.
- Ratio analysis. Monitor levels of solvency and liquidity through the application of ratio analysis specifically relating to working capital management.

Marketing

Marketing is a massive area full of specialists who have worked in the field for years and who are still learning and developing their craft, so I won't try to give you a definitive guide to marketing. This chapter acts as a basic guideline to marketing concepts of which the small business owner/manager should be aware. It will also demonstrate how management accounting and marketing go hand in hand.

The aim of marketing is to achieve the right balance to deliver efficiently and profitably a product wanted by the customer. You don't need to be a seasoned marketeer to accomplish this objective.

The relevance of management accounting to marketing

It is rarely thought that marketing and accounting functions should work closely together. There is often a perception in businesses that accounting is largely irrelevant to what the marketing department do, as it is rarely appreciated just how much the two areas of business are reliant upon each other to maximise both their potential. However, it is important to see these two areas of business provide each other data to produce information which will improve the financial performance of the company as a whole.

So, how can these functions work to help each other and how can the transfer of good-quality information create better overall company information and performance? Management accounting working with marketing can produce:

- better financial data for product pricing based on suitable decision-making techniques;
- an understanding of the financial performance of the company, which may impact on a marketing budget resulting in spending constraints;
- more detailed customer information to aid pricing and promotion decisions;
- knowing the real value of brand equity;
- the financial impact of a brand strategy – in terms of both turnover and profits;
- product life cycles and the relationship with the company's working capital – what you need to do versus what you can afford to do.

Immediate benefits can be achieved once management accounting is embraced as part of the marketing remit within an SME.

Specific marketing techniques

In this chapter, we will look in detail at four of the most important management accounting techniques for marketing, which are:

1. marketing mix (Four Ps);
2. brand equity and valuation;
3. product life cycle;
4. competitive strategy.

The marketing mix (Four Ps)

The Four Ps of the marketing mix are product, place, price and promotion. It is a combination of these four elements that will maximise sales and profit potential.

1. Product

Think about what you are selling and why. Ensure that your product is sufficiently original or better than competitors' products to ensure that it will capture the desired market share. It's important to think about your product from a customer's perspective. Imagine yourself as a member of the target market and ask yourself – would you actually use this product? Hopefully by now your market research should be signalling that the market needs or wants this product.

During the development of your product, it is essential to keep in mind who your customers are and what their demands are. People can be generalised and defined into categories through demographic profiling. Make sure you know your market!

You know what your customers want today, but you should also aim to anticipate how their wants and needs may change in the future. Consider the environment in which your target market operates. Know this environment as well as you know the people inside it. Keep up to date with what is going on in terms of trends, developments and competitors' products.

Finally, ensure that your product satisfies the needs of your target customer base. Give them what they want. If you don't, you could be in for an expensive education campaign that may not have the desired effect. As we saw in Chapter 2, SMEs rarely have the working capital for this level of marketing and advertising, so it can often be better to approach a market where there is existing demand. Introducing a new product to an untried market can sometimes be worth the gamble, provided it is a well-planned strategy based on well-researched behavioural patterns.

2. Place

Ensure that customers can access your product. The availability of the product and the distribution channels to be used can make a very big difference to the successful marketing of the product and the profitability of the business.

The product must be available to meet the demands of the customer. It should be situated in a place where a customer would reasonably expect to find it without too much effort. If a customer has to try to find the product, it is likely that they will give up and buy an alternative that is easier to source.

Outsourcing the distribution process can be a cost-effective and efficient way for an SME to ensure that a product reaches its market. Distributors should be based locally, or at least have excellent knowledge of the target geographic or demographic data. They will sell you their expertise and their contacts, usually for a reasonably high percentage of turnover or profit. A distributor's fees can sometimes be the single largest cost of sale of a business. However, consider the cost of creating and operating an international sales force and doing your own marketing in a market where you have little or no experience, not to mention the difficulties of stock and credit control. Outsourcing works, and it can be extremely valuable for the small start-up as well as for multinational corporations.

Distributors, both domestic and international, should be expected to provide the company with an annual sales forecast, which is generally rationalised for the purposes of the company sales budget. Remember that distributors are salespeople, so their figures should be reviewed to ensure that they are realistic. From their fee, the distributors should be expected to cover marketing, movement of stock, and customer care, including retailer questions. A good distributor should also deal with any problems at source to protect the brand and then pass on this information to the company. If managed effectively, a distribution system works and ensures that the company enjoys a much wider audience.

3. Price

Your pricing should be attractive to customers while ensuring that your company makes a profit. Consider your methodology for pricing, as there are many and varied ways of approaching how to set the retail or wholesale price for your product. First, ensure that you know all relevant fixed and variable costs, such as raw materials, labour, production, warehousing and carriage – anything that is spent on the direct creation of your product to bring it to a marketable and saleable state. This is the basis of information you need to make even the most basic pricing decision.

Pricing methodologies

There are several approaches to pricing, depending on the product and process involved to deliver the product to the market.

Case studies

When setting up Telecoms Co, the pricing model was largely dictated by the industry and market, specifically the price perception of the customer. In wholesale telecoms, as with many businesses, there is an expected level of pricing that the customer will accept. The pricing was therefore calculated based on the margin usually accepted in the industry, in this case between 0.5 and 1p per minute, depending on the quality of route (product). This is called *market-based pricing*. If they had priced higher than the market dictated there would have been little or, more likely, no customer take-up.

Alternatively, Bed Co developed their pricing model based on competition. However, this has been a discussion point in the business where the two directors don't see eye to eye. The debate is whether they should price around the competition and take a smaller margin or price the product as a luxury item (which it is perceived by the customer to be) and hope that their target market see the value in paying more for a better product. This current model is called *competitive pricing*, whereas the proposed method is referred to as *premium pricing*.

In this case, there is no right or wrong answer. First, pricing should be based on what a customer will pay for a product. However, there are always secondary motives which will affect how much a company should charge the customer. For Bed Co, the secondary factor will be the outcome of the objectives of the company in terms of profitability and how they want their product to be perceived in the marketplace.

There is a strong argument from recent studies into purchasing behaviour that consumers will pay substantially more if a product is perceived to be of a higher quality than its competitors. The product is perceived at a higher quality because it costs more and consumers are happy to pay this premium. An example of this is organic food products, for which customers pay a high premium, though the actual benefits of organic food are not always clear or understood.

Another method that is popular for small businesses is the *cost-plus price method*, whereby you would add up all of the costs that go into making a product (the variable costs) and calculate a margin that will cover the overheads (fixed costs) of the business and provide a desirable pre-tax profit.

Pricing – the simple approach for SMEs

An easy approach to develop a price for your product is to apply the following simple equation:

$$P = (C + D + V) + (F/Q)$$

where:

P = price per unit
C = per unit commissions, discounts
D = per unit distribution, agency, carriage costs
V = all other per unit variable costs (excluding C and D)
Q = total number of units sold
F = total fixed costs.

When applying this formula, it is important to remember to start with known variable costs. Consider every expense item that is needed to provide your product to market – labour, manufacturing, storage, packaging, labelling, distribution, discounts, marketing – the list is a long one, so make sure you capture all of the costs to price correctly. Do not include 'sunk costs'. These are costs which have already been borne by the company and should not be factored into any ongoing, future pricing analysis.

The price should be calculated on a per unit basis and should include a proportion of the total fixed cost (overheads) per unit in the price. This is called 'overhead absorption' and will be covered in more detail in Chapter 6.

The reason for using overhead absorption is that sales should not just cover direct (variable) costs but should also contribute sufficiently towards fixed costs (overheads) to provide the company with an overall profit. Gross profit is sometimes called 'contribution', as it is the profit generated by the normal operations of the company which contributes towards covering the overheads with an aim of generating an overall profit for the business.

When you have a unit price for the product based on your internal figures, compare this price with that of the competitors and other similar products in the market. If your product is £4 more than the competition, ask yourself if there is an obvious differentiator for which a customer would be happy to pay a premium.

The preferred pricing method will depend on your profit motives and market forces.

4. Promotion

Ensure that customers know about your product through effective advertising. Customer awareness should also ensure that they know correct and complete information about your product and/or your company.

Whether it is more appropriate to lead the advertising campaign with your company or your product depends on your product. This should be an obvious decision point; however, where it is not, decide which of the two is more appealing and easier to understand.

Case study

Bath Co is an example of leading with a brand first and then the products second. The brand is the core of all advertising and promotion, with the design capturing attention. The products then back this up. Conversely, Telecoms Co lead with the product as the brand or the name of the company itself is largely irrelevant to the product that they offer. Indeed, they have changed the company name twice without significantly changing the product offering and/or customer base.

The Four Ps are a good source of planning to create a brief marketing plan. This is usually a formal strategy document, either for the business plan or for internal purposes, and is an extremely useful activity for clarity of action. This will ensure that you have the right product, at the right price, and that your target market can find out sufficient information about the product, which encourages them to become a customer. This plan will also save the company time and money now and in the future with regard to marketing spend, which can easily become an uncontrolled business cost.

Brand equity and valuation

A brand provides the product with identification to the market and can be in the form of a word, symbol or design which is unique and specific to that product. History shows that branding is a critical part of the initial success and longevity of a product within the market.

Brand equity is a management accounting concept that allows the brand to be considered and treated as an asset. It is quite understandable to treat a brand as an asset, as it provides the company with a benefit that is expected to increase shareholders' wealth.

Valuation of a brand

A straightforward method of valuing a brand is to establish how much was spent on its development. This valuation, however, can be misleading owing to the changing time value of money. It is therefore recommended to perform a net present value (NPV) analysis, which is covered in Chapter 5. An NPV calculation will correct this distortion of time.

Other methods of brand valuation include:

- estimating what another company would pay for the brand;
- keeping profit and loss accounts for each brand;
- calculating marketing expenditure to date and future spend projections to the maturity stage of the product life cycle;
- brand performance information such as market share and customer loyalty.

Brand accounting for SMEs

Considering the brand as an asset of the company has its problems, the main one being measurement. How to measure intangible assets has given accountants a challenge since the concept of capitalising a 'brand' was created and recognised on the balance sheet in the 1980s. The term 'capitalising' refers to the recognition of an item of expenditure on the balance sheet as an asset rather than writing it to the profit and loss account as an expense.

In general, and for accounting purposes of an SME, the expenditure made on a brand should be treated as an intangible asset when another business has been acquired. This balance sheet item should then be amortised over the perceived life of the brand. Amortisation is an accounting entry which writes down the value of an intangible asset to the profit and loss account.

For example, £100,000 was spent on the acquisition of a brand. It is envisaged that the brand will fall into the 'neglect' stage of the product life cycle after 10 years. The balance sheet, which starts off with £100,000 as an asset, should then decrease in value each year over 10 years, with the amortisation being recognised in the profit and loss statement each year.

There remains an element of controversy over whether or not so-called 'home grown' brands should be capitalised. For many companies, this approach by Financial Reporting Standard 10 (FRS10) doesn't make accounting sense as, for many companies, a brand has the effect of enhancing sales over the long term of the business, which is the very definition of an asset.

Product life cycle

Developing a product life cycle is relevant to overall business planning as flexible marketing tactics are required throughout the life of any product. This means that different information is required through the application of management accounting models, upon the output of which product development and marketing decisions will be made.

CIMA defines the product life cycle as 'the period which begins with the initial product specification, and ends with the withdrawal from the market of both the product and its support. It is characterised by defined stages including research, development, introduction, maturity, decline and abandonment.'

As most companies provide a number of different products, it is essential to look at the profitability and marketability of each product separately. The product life cycle (Figure 3.1) helps in understanding how a product is used in the market, which will drive many internal decisions such as development, marketing and overhead apportionment.

Stages of the product life cycle

There are five stages to the product life cycle – introduction, growth, maturity, decline and neglect.

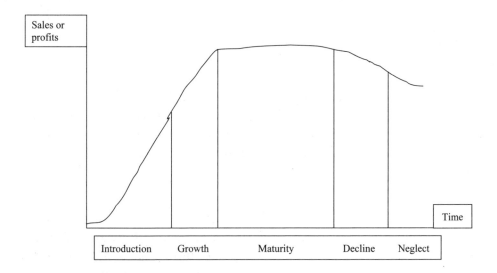

Figure 3.1   Product life cycle

1. Introduction

Sales growth is slow in the introduction period as brand awareness is created. This is a high-risk and expensive time in the life of a product as the marketing effort to reach the customer base is imperative. The education of new customers and stealing a competitor's current market share are strategies in this phase of the product life cycle.

2. Growth

There is an opportunity to grow the product as product awareness is increased and the product sees a lift in customer uptake. Sales, and therefore profits, will increase unless the product is a loss leader, in which case the company should monitor the sales level and correct the pricing to a profitable level when appropriate. This is also a time of weakness, as competitors are alerted to a new product gaining strength and are likely to create barriers to further growth.

3. Maturity

This stage sees a slowdown in market share and growth as the product reaches maturity. This is generally the longest period in a product's life, and can range from months to decades, depending on the volatility of the market in which it is sold. This is generally a profitable stage of the product, as brand awareness is high and marketing is not required to educate the market, but merely to retain a level of awareness.

4. Decline

New entrants to the market or increased market share to existing competitors will result in a decline in the demand of a product. This could be due to an oversupply of similar products or a cheaper alternative provided to customers who, in general, are only loyal while it makes economic sense for them to be so.

5. Neglect

When competition is too fierce or customer demand falls away so that it is no longer profitable to make a product, it falls into a stage of neglect. At this stage a product may be left to fall out of the market on its own, or it may be completely withdrawn and destroyed. Most companies feel reluctant to leave a market completely; however, brand perception must be considered and if a product is seriously underperforming, one must consider the overall brand and withdraw the product.

The benefit of analysing product life cycles is a more effective control over costs. Purchasing and resource management can be better controlled if it is known when new products are required or when demand for existing products will slow.

Competitive strategy

Define your competitive strategy from environmental analysis carried out in your business plan and subsequent reviews. This process is covered in Chapter 5 in more detail. The section on stakeholders in Chapter 1 is also relevant to the competitive strategy process. It is essential to know who your competitors are, as it is these companies who will have the biggest external influence on your company's marketing strategy. We will cover strategy in more detail in Chapter 5.

According to business and marketing strategist Michael Porter, there are three main strategic options – cost leader, differentiator and niche market positions:

- cost leader – being able to produce a product for the lowest cost compared with other companies in your industry;
- differentiator – providing a product that is perceived as being sufficiently unique and thereby warranting a higher price premium;
- niche – focusing on a segment of the market that has a true appreciation of your product. There is often higher brand loyalty for niche products, yet the market is smaller. SMEs often aim for niche products as it is generally cheaper to reach and communicate the Four Ps to a niche market.

Know your enemy

When setting your marketing strategy, ensure that your competitor analysis has been carried out, with particular attention to how they approach their strategy. It is often easier to obtain information about your competitor than you may think, as there is an assumed link between their strategy and their cost structure. Sources of this type of information include published accounts, trading history with customers and suppliers, published marketing strategy and public announcements.

Answering some of the following questions may give you valuable insight into your competitor. Does your competitor have a higher fixed cost base to cover through higher pricing? Are there any constraints over supply that is different from your company? Do they have access to a wider market, and how?

Gather and filter through as much data as possible and apply the specifics of your competitors' business against your own business models to gain a greater insight into their strategies.

Barriers to entry

Competitors will often try to keep other new entrants out of their industry or will try to limit the market share that existing companies are seeking to claim. They do this by setting up barriers to entry to limit the threat from their competition.

'Barriers to entry' is one of the 'five competitive forces', which is a tool for developing strategy, as covered in Chapter 4. Barriers to entry include:

- Economies of scale. The purchasing power that comes from buying higher quantities from suppliers may not be available to smaller new entrants. Should an existing competitor be able to keep costs low through economies of scale, the cost saving is likely to result in a lower sales price per unit, which will impact on customer behaviour towards their competitor.
- Capital requirements. Investment from a new or expanding entrant to a market is likely to be high risk and therefore may be more expensive to finance. If capital requirements are high, the barrier to new entrants could be prohibitive.
- Access to suppliers. Supplier agreements may be difficult to establish and new entrants to a market may have poorer contractual terms than an existing customer. A supplier may require pro forma (up-front) payment or may not extend certain discounts or incentives that are provided to companies who are seen as low risk owing to their established credit history. This can have a negative impact on both profits and working capital.
- Access to customers. Customers need to be convinced to move away from one product to start using another. Generally, a new entrant

cannot afford to provide discounts or incentives to customers to start using their product over that of a competitor. High marketing costs together with promotion and placement access can create barriers to certain markets. One example is CTNs (confectioners, tobacconists and newsagents), who have very limited shelf and counter space. They will only give precious space to products that are proven to be in demand by customers and that also give them the biggest commissions. It is very difficult for a new entrant to convince a shop owner to take a chance on them for a few months to prove their product.

■ Product perception. Customers tend to have a certain amount of brand loyalty. A new product in the market must educate and convince customers in the market to use their product. This can be a timely and expensive process. To further prevent new competition, existing customers may promote several brands, which has the effect of crowding the market.

While the best competitive strategy option will be dependent on your market and industry, it is important to define your strategy and stick with it. It is often the case that a company that tries to mix strategies will not be as successful as a company that has committed to a predetermined strategic direction.

Conclusion

Marketing can benefit from management accounting techniques and the two departments or functions within a company should stop being strangers or even enemies. The successful integration and communication of ideas, data and information will ensure a more efficient company.

As SMEs often find resources tight owing to financial constraints, it is more important that all information available is used to optimum efficiency. The output from the techniques used will be enhanced by the level of accurate data fed into the models from all areas of the company. This can only be done through effective communication.

Key points to remember

Marketing and accounting should work closely together to benefit the efficiency of the overall company.

- ■ Specific marketing techniques include:
  - Marketing mix (Four Ps):
    - Product.
    - Place.
    - Price.
    - Promotion.
  - Brand equity and valuation.
  - Product life cycle:
    - Introduction.
    - Growth.
    - Maturity.
    - Decline.
    - Neglect.
  - Competitive strategy:
    - Three key competitive strategies are:
      - Cost leader.
      - Differentiator.
      - Niche.
    - Know your enemy.
    - Barriers to entry:
      - Economies of scale.
      - Capital requirements.
      - Access to suppliers.
      - Access to customers.
      - Product perception.

Planning and budgeting

None of us knows what is going to happen in the future. If we did, we'd all be jetting off to our private islands. While we mere mortals may not have the benefit of hindsight, we can greatly improve our situations with good analysis, research and forward planning.

Many of the events that happen to a small business should be able to be planned for in advance. Management should capture data, extrapolate its usefulness and use this information to see into the future. Of course, not all events can be planned based on historic data and educated guesswork. All SME owners/managers can do is to use the resources that they have available to them to best predict future events. The skill is in knowing which data will provide this precious information and how to understand what it is trying to communicate.

Why budget?

Any business that operates without a budget is not operating as efficiently as possible and is therefore losing money. Budgeting is a method of protecting the assets and resources of the company while maximising the benefits to be gained from them.

Budgeting for a company's activities will provide the following benefits:

- control over resources;

- improved allocation and use of resources;
- increased efficiency translates into increased profitability;
- improved environmental awareness;
- maintain competitive advantage;
- reduce uncertainty on specific events;
- ability to capitalise on identified opportunities;
- basis for analysis against actual performance;
- variance analysis provide tools for management decision making.

There are many different levels of budgeting, depending on the size and complexity of the company. While the principles and benefits remain the same, the style of budget should be adapted to suit the operational activities and objectives set by management for the company.

The relevance of management accounting to budgeting

The Chartered Institute of Management Accountants' (CIMA) official terminology for a budget is 'a quantitative statement, for a defined period of time, which may include planned revenues, expenses, assets, liabilities and cashflows. A budget provides a focus for the organisation, aids the coordination of activities and facilitates control. Planning is achieved by means of a fixed master budget, whereas control is generally exercised through the comparison of actual costs with a flexible budget.'

Management accounting uses the budget to look at the entire operations of the company with the goal of improving efficiency and thereby maximising shareholder value – the ultimate operational role and legal obligation of the directors of the company.

Budgeting is more than numbers on a spreadsheet to guide the company. The analysis that is carried out from the budgeted financial performance is why management accounting techniques are critical to using budgeting effectively within a corporate environment. Before creating a budget, the company must be sure of its objectives as the budget is built upon realising these through the achievement of a series of goals.

Set company objectives

Each company is different owing to the industry, the market and the environment in which it operates. Budgeting should be flexible based on the individual needs of the company and its management.

First, be aware of the objectives of the company. What are you hoping to achieve through and from the budgeting process? Strategic objectives are set by directors or management as a plan for the operations of the business to follow. Some key strategic objectives may include:

- Greater control of resources.
- Ability to understand the financial performance of the company – how well did the company do over a fixed period.
- Planning of allocation of resources.
- Is the balance sheet supporting the P&L – ie is there a sufficient asset base with working capital to generate the required profits?

These are often the top four strategic objectives from management when setting out to create a budget that will meet their needs. The majority of small companies would benefit from the use of objectives as a starting point, from which to add their own, more bespoke trading targets.

Objectives are the driving force of the business and the intentions behind every action that the business makes to operate in a certain way towards a particular outcome. Objectives should be clear, concise and should work together towards the same overall corporate aim. This goal congruence should be a feature of all objectives set within the company.

For example, if there is a predetermined objective to increase profit, the goal of sales should be to sell more units and the aim of purchasing is to buy cheaper. This meeting of minds is called goal congruence.

There cannot always be such clear goal congruence with objectives. When there is a genuine conflict of actions, a primary and secondary objective must be determined by management. It is the primary objective that takes priority over the secondary. In practice, however, it is often the case that two conflicting objectives cannot be so clearly categorised in this fashion.

For example, the management of a company may wish to retain working capital for a new project which will net a substantial profit. Use of debt financing would be prohibitively expensive and therefore management have decided to use retained profits to fund the venture. The shareholders, however, have an objective to realise a certain return on investment through the taking of dividends, which are distributed from retained profits. Here there is a clear conflict. The shareholders ultimately have the power over the distribution of profits; however, it may be the case that the value of the business will be improved should the project be allowed to go ahead through the funding from internally generated working capital. In this case, negotiations and further analysis would occur, as there is no clear primary and secondary objective.

The SMART acronym is often used to describe the key characteristics of quantifiable objectives:

Specific
Measurable
Attainable
Results-oriented
Time-bounded

I would add four more significant attributes, as understanding the importance of objectives is the foundation stage to the construction of the business. Objectives should also be:

Focused
Agreed between shareholders, directors and managers – where possible
Communicated to the company as a whole – staff looking at big picture
Efficient

From this foundation of setting clear objectives, the strategy is then developed, upon which the operations are put into place and the business is expected to return full circle to meet the corporate objectives (Figure 4.1). It is, therefore, essential to set clear, purposeful objectives to guide the success of the company.

Determine the short- and long-term objectives of the company and ensure that they meet the above characteristics. Once strategic objectives have been agreed, look at how the financial performance of the company can work to help these objectives to be realised. There are many financial objectives that are relevant to an SME.

Profitability

Consider the profit motive in conjunction with other objectives. Looking at profit on its own can distort the big picture; for example, perhaps it is

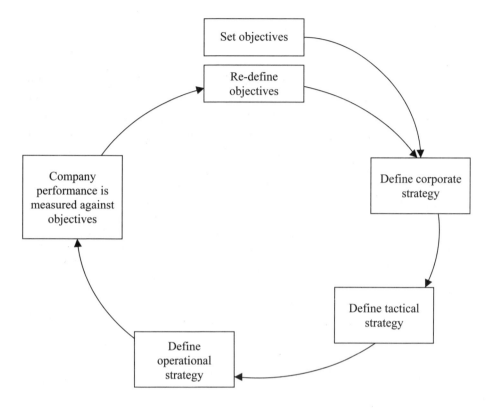

Figure 4.1   Objectives full circle

better to make less profit this year to capture a greater market share that will see increased profits in future periods. Profitability does not take into consideration capital investment required for such projects.

Return on capital employed (ROCE)

ROCE should be one of the key performance indicators on your management accounting pack (MAP), as covered in Chapter 6. The ROCE should be a primary objective of the company. Bear in mind certain considerations when determining your ROCE objectives, which is calculated as profits as a percentage of capital employed. Also expressed as:

$$\frac{\text{Earnings before interest and tax}}{\text{Total assets} - \text{current liabilities}}$$

Data used should be consistent by ensuring that the figures used each time the ROCE is calculated are produced using the same method. For example, if net present value (NPV) is used to value the assets for the calculation instead of net replacement cost, then this should always be so. Remember that one of the key characteristics of an objective is that it is measurable.

Dividend policy

Shareholders will consider the return on their investment when reviewing investment options. Dividend growth will be a likely objective of the shareholder and therefore should be a primary objective of the managers of the company, as a director's fiduciary duty is to increase shareholders' wealth, which was discussed in Chapter 1 and will be covered again in Chapter 12.

Ensure that the objectives selected for your company meet the above criteria. They should first be strategic and then have a financial or operational focus. Document these objectives clearly as they will now go on to form the basis of the strategic and planning review.

Strategic and planning review

Before setting out to construct the actual budget, a thorough strategic and planning review of the business and its activities should be carried out to ensure that the budget captures all relevant data. The budget should build on the information gleaned from this relevant data. The business planning activity should provide an updated analysis based on reliable information, which will become the content of the final budget.

Strategy is all about deciding on a course of action, based on agreed objectives. Start by going back to basics. Ask yourself what the company is good at and whether or not it is delivering on these skills, or are the resources of the company being used to maintain other activities. Use the objectives to drive the strategic thinking and review.

When commencing a strategic review, management must consider the following questions:

- What actions should be implemented to meet objectives?
- What is customer demand and how can the business deliver customer satisfaction?
- What are the strengths and weaknesses of the business?
- What trends lie behind market conditions?
- Where is the balance between risk and reward?

Case study

When the TravelCo directors set up their company, they had a clear idea of what they wanted to achieve in terms of sales and profits, though no clear picture on how they were going to achieve these objectives. Objectives are essential, as is a clear path of actions to achieve the objectives. I worked with the directors to turn their one-page strategic objective document into a strategic plan which looked at the environment in which the company would operate, ie the travel industry, and the internal resources. It was clear after a small amount of planning that they would not achieve their objectives with the resources they were planning to have available. They had to decide between changing their objectives and altering the resource planning to meet the existing objectives. They chose to make some changes to the labour resource and overhead budget to be able to meet their strategic objectives. The planning exercise was important for them to realise what was required operationally to meet the strategic objectives. The result was that the actual performance was in line with the budget, which stemmed from the strategic review.

The next step in the budget process is to carry out environmental analysis, which will start to answer some of the questions asked. While we introduced this concept during the business planning stage, a thorough strategic review requires more detail and structure. Environmental analysis at this level requires defined structure, which is provided by four management accounting techniques proven to benefit the SME:

1. PEST analysis;
2. SWOT analysis;

3. gap analysis;
4. Porter's five forces analysis.

The owner/manager of a small business should have an awareness of all of these methods; however, not all of the detail of each will be relevant to every business. The key is to identify those areas of each model that relate to your business and apply the theory to a strategic review as part of the budget process. Simply address each point below and ask how it is, or could be, relevant to your company.

PEST analysis

A PEST analysis is a review of the political, economic, social and technological factors in the external environment in which all companies operate. All companies should carry out PEST analysis at an early stage in the life of the company and update this analysis annually or when significant changes occur within the environment. PEST factors tend to be country specific and should therefore be carried out on all countries in which the company has significant operations.

Political factors include:

- workplace health and safety issues;
- stability of government;
- change of political leader or party;
- pricing regulations;
- labour legislation, such as minimum wage and employee benefits;
- changes to contract law;
- product requirements, such as regulation of labelling or contents;
- taxation – rate increases/decreases or change to compliance regulations.

Economic factors include:

- unemployment rates;
- interest rates;
- rate of inflation;
- exchange rate fluctuations;
- rate and direction of economic growth;

- labour cost and availability of different skill levels;
- comparative advantages of the UK against home countries of competitors;
- type of economic model in country, ie free market.

Social factors include:

- education;
- culture;
- demographic profile;
- approach to business ethics;
- behaviour and habits of customer base;
- attitude towards merit and entrepreneurialism.

Technological factors include:

- rate of technological advancement;
- new developments of technology;
- impact of technology on the product or its delivery to market.

As you can see, there are many external factors to consider about the environment in which a company operates. As there are so many issues to consider, an SME should prioritise the most important and relevant economic factors that relate to the business. While this review is seen as an important part of the strategic review process, it will undoubtedly require some managerial assumptions as there may be a degree of uncertainty about the data. The PEST analysis, therefore, should always be used in conjunction with other analyses.

SWOT analysis

Every corporate strategic review should include a SWOT analysis, which considers the internal and external factors of a company's strengths, weaknesses, opportunities and threats. Strengths and weaknesses are an internal appraisal of the company and its operations, whereas opportunities and threats focus on the business environment (external).

When carrying out a SWOT analysis, consider the opinion of as many people in your company as is practical to include. Employees and contractors will have a different point of view on their area of operations and business perspective. Management should generate the outline of the SWOT analysis and distribute it accordingly for a wider input before it is finalised. As the outline will ideally pass through many hands, it is a good idea to create a clear template to facilitate input from multiple parties.

Figure 4.2 shows a common format for the SWOT analysis. This example uses some general business issues; however, your specific business is likely to have different or even unique issues that will need to be addressed for each square.

Once the SWOT analysis has had input from management and staff, use the data to identify areas that could be improved or changed. For example, if manufacturing bottleneck issues have been raised by those on the production line, management should investigate to see if the situation could be easily resolved. If the solution is not simple, this should be factored into any further productivity analysis and a longer-term solution established.

Gap analysis

Gap analysis is an analytical tool which enables a company to compare its objectives (such as profitability or growth) with its expected performance. The output from this analysis highlights areas that require improvement by the management of the company. The process of gap analysis involves calculating the variance between business requirements and current resource availability and potential.

Remember to use the company's current resources to plan the expected performance. It is important to use this current data to provide the planning gap as it will ultimately provide more realistic information.

One of the most popular applications of gap analysis is the profit gap (Figure 4.3). This is calculated as the difference between target profits (objective) and the profits on the forecast. Bear in mind that the forecast profit is that which would be made if the company continued on its existing operational path using available resources. The gap is the amount which needs to be 'filled' by a change in strategic or operational direction to achieve the original objective.

Management accounting practice suggests that gap analysis can be carried out on most areas of the business, such as working capital, production, labour resource availability and efficiency and asset usage. The output from the analysis tool provides a platform for measuring the efficiency and availability of specific resources required to achieve the company's objectives.

Strengths	Weaknesses
Examples include:	*Examples include:*
· Competitive advantage	· Cashflow constraints
· Innovative aspects of product range	· Supply chain issues
· Marketing distribution and price	· Poor organisational management
· Quality of resources such as people or assets	· Insufficient processes and systems
Opportunities	**Threats**
Examples include:	*Examples include:*
· New markets	· Loss of key labour resource
· Agency or distribution network	· Competitor strength and motives
· Economies of scale	· IT developments
· Seasonal influences	· Market demand

Figure 4.2   SWOT analysis

Note: the above table has used examples of each category – strengths, weaknesses, opportunities and threats – that may apply to a small business. Not all of these examples will apply to every business.

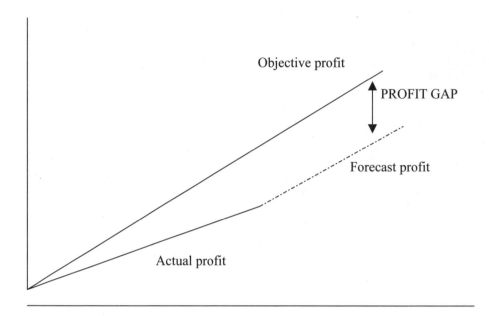

Figure 4.3 Profit gap chart

Porter's five forces analysis

Before looking at the five forces model, remember that it is an all-encompassing model aimed at larger companies. Having said that, there are still benefits for the SME to carry out this analysis as it does provide valuable information from the analysis it requires.

For SMEs, the five forces model is a tool I would suggest using near the beginning of a company's life or for guidance leading up to a change in strategy – planned or otherwise. It is also a useful exercise to carry out during a period of instability.

The idea behind the model is that, if a company expects to be competitive, it must be well armed to combat each of the five competitive forces. It assumes a relatively hostile environment, as is often the reality in a competitive industry. It implies that it is better to be over-prepared than ill-equipped. On this basis, approach the model with a defensive view of the company's environment.

The five competitive forces in the model are (Figure 4.4):

- the threat of new entrants to the industry;
- the threat of a substitute product;

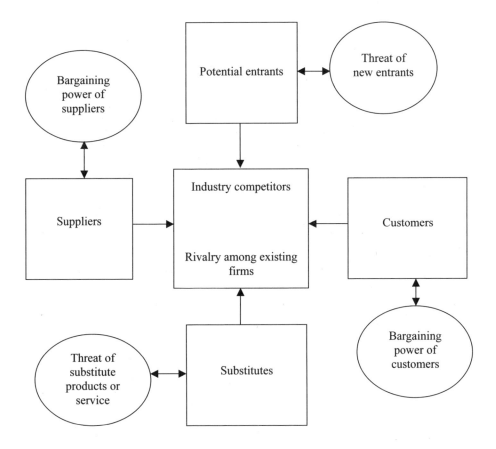

Figure 4.4 Porter's five forces

Source: CIMA Business Strategy (adapted from Porter: Competitive Strategy)

- the bargaining power of customers;
- the bargaining power of suppliers;
- the rivalry among competitors in the industry.

Let's look briefly at each of these forces in turn.

The threat of new entrants to the industry

Review factors that may act as barriers to entry, such as economies of scale which are enjoyed by competitors. A few business assumptions based on recent research, combined with general enquiries to suppliers regarding pricing discounts for purchasing levels, should enable management to quantify the level of barrier this creates for the new entrant. Capital requirements may also be prohibitively high, such as start-up production materials and equipment. Existing companies may also sweeten current deals with their customers to encourage them to stay rather than switch over to a different provider of the product.

The threat of a substitute product

Customers want their needs satisfied. If a substitute product is introduced into the market which can satisfy their needs better or for less, there is a risk that customers will move to the new entrant. Maintain an awareness of new developments and technologies which may enable substitute products to be more efficiently produced and/or delivered to market.

The bargaining power of customers

Customer strength largely depends on their demand for the product, the competitiveness of the industry and most of all what proportion of total sales of your company they comprise. It may sound obvious, but try to reduce the strength of your customers to maintain the balance of power in the company's favour. One key way of doing this is to ensure a good spread of customers within the company. The general rule of thumb on this is that one customer should not equal more than 10 per cent of turnover. If they do, they are seen as being in a position of strength and this power should be considered a threat. This concept ties in with Pareto analysis that we will cover in Chapter 5.

Also, consider how critical the product is to the customer's own business and their level of profitability, which is reliant upon buying from you at a certain price. While they could be 25 per cent of your company's sales, the customer may need your product as much as you need their sales. Know the balance of power with each main customer.

The bargaining power of suppliers

Suppliers can often exert power over SMEs, as they will often compare small companies with larger companies and give favourable pricing or discounts based on larger order quantities. Being a small fish in a big pond can reduce your company's bargaining power. Try to acquire as much information as possible about the supplier's customer base and their business to establish the threat level. Taking the time to find the right suppliers for your business can be an effective competitive strategy.

The rivalry among competitors in the industry

Before entering an industry, identify the key companies and their objectives and strategies. It may be that you have to play them at their own game to compete, or alternatively provide a product with sufficient differentiation so that you are not in direct competition.

Once the analysis of these five forces has been applied to your business, management should be better prepared to combat threats from the environment. Do your research – better the devil you know.

Different types of budget

We will next take a look at the different types of budget, not all of which will be relevant or suitable for your company's financial, management or operational structure. Choose the method that is best suited for your business and its successful application will provide the information required to meet your corporate objectives.

There are many formats that the company budget could take. Deciding on the most appropriate budget format will rely on a number of factors, including:

- size and complexity of your business;
- resources available to produce and maintain the budget;
- stage of growth of the company (start-up to mature business);
- industry in which the company operates;
- type of product offered by the company.

Let's start by looking at traditional budgeting and then branch out into specific budgeting styles that may be more appropriate to your specific business.

Traditional budgeting

Traditional budgeting usually uses the actual data from the previous year, along with the variance analysis, to identify any previous planning weaknesses or areas where the company did not perform in line with budget. This data, along with management knowledge and experience, provides the basis on which a budget for the following period can be built.

The budget for the next period is then developed using a combination of three main components:

- historical data;
- information gained about future events;
- assumptions relating to unknown issues that will impact on operations or performance.

The format of a traditional budget normally reflects the format of the reported primary financial statements, which allows for simple comparison of actual financial performance against the budget. Chapter 6 suggests a format for the primary financial statements which are appropriate for SMEs. These financial statements (ie profit and loss statement and balance sheet) then become the framework upon which the budget information is reported.

Traditional budgeting involves the whole of the company, in as much detail as possible, as each area of responsibility will impact on its overall financial performance.

Incremental budgeting

Incremental budgeting takes historic, actual data from the previous period and makes a mark up (or down) depending on how management anticipate the company should perform in the next period. For example, if sales in 2006 were £100,000, and management felt that 2007 should see a 5 per cent uplift in total sales, then the sales budget for 2007 would be £105,000 (calculated by applying the incremental factor to the historic data, ie £100,000 * 1.05).

The theory applies to all elements throughout the profit and loss statement to provide incremental income and expense figures. This method is flawed for many businesses as it does not take any other factors into consideration, such as the introduction of a new product or one-off events that may occur in one year but not the next. It should also be said that this method does not consider the behaviour of customers and suppliers and other market forces which may impact on the profitability of the company.

The term 'logical incrementalism' is often used to describe this approach to business planning as it assumes that there is an underlying logic behind the incremental data. Percentage increases or decreases should be based on well-researched data, management logic and information. The emphasis on management knowledge and logic underlies the importance of information systems, as covered in Chapter 9, and of organisational management, as covered in Chapter 7. Both knowledge capture and its communication are key to budgeting accurately.

For businesses that operate in a very stable trading environment, and that do not plan any radical developments to their company, this method is a straightforward, cost-effective way of budgeting.

Profit-motive-based budgeting

While not a recognised formal approach to budgeting, I find that this method works for many small businesses in a practical sense. I have found that when people either start up a business or look to budget for an existing business, it is fairly certain that they have a profit expectation. Management should generally have an idea of either the profit (gross or operating) percentage or fixed amount that they require from their business. This absolute figure or percentage is then used as the starting point for the budget.

Once you have an accurate profit figure in mind, start building the budget around this figure. Let's use a fixed operating profit objective for the following example of building a profit-motive-based budget.

The owner of A Ltd knows she wants to achieve an operating profit of £50,000 for the year 2008, up from £35,000 in the previous year. For the purposes of her budget, operating profit is EBITDA, which is the commonly used acronym for earnings before interest, tax, depreciation and amortisation.

She knows that her overheads were around £75,000 in 2007 and are unlikely to change much, apart from one further staff member required for the full year at £20,000 and an increase in rent and property charges totalling £5,000. This puts her total budgeted overhead expenditure at £100,000 for 2008.

The owner is sure that her gross profitability will not change from 2007 to 2008, therefore cost of sales will remain at 55 per cent. We can now calculate the required sales figure. Add the required operating profit of £50,000 to the expected overheads of £100,000, giving a required gross profit of £150,000. If cost of sales is steady at 55 per cent of sales, then gross profit must be

45 per cent (the balancing figure). Take the gross profit of £150,000 and divide it by the gross profit percentage of sales: £150,000 / 0.45 = £333,333. We now know that the company must achieve sales of £333,333 to produce an operating profit of £50,000. This sales figure becomes the budget to achieve the financial objective of the operating profit.

Let's look at the budgeted P&L for A Ltd for 2008 alongside the actuals for 2007 (Figure 4.5).

	2007	2008	
Sales	244,444	333,333	Calculate up from operating profit objective to find required sales budget
Cost of sales (55%)	134,444	183,333	
Gross profit	110,000	150,000	
Overheads	75,000	100,000	
Operating profit	35,000	50,000	

Figure 4.5 Profit-motive-based budgeting (A Ltd)

This theory can be applied using either the gross or operating profit. In the example above we have used the operating profit to calculate up (sales, cost of sales and overheads). If your gross profit figure is the clearer objective, use this as the starting point and work up (sales and cost of sales) and down (overheads and other relevant costs) to achieve your desired planning outcome.

This theory works well with relatively simple business operations where the driving factor is a certain level of desired profitability.

Activity-based budgeting

Activity-based budgeting (ABB) is a method of budgeting based on the operations of a company – what it actually does as the activity which generates income. For example, if the company is a real estate agency, the operational objective is to sell enough properties to make the entity profitable. In this case, the activity is selling property. ABB will then focus on the sales units of the company, which will act as the key driver for the budget. This means that all other components of the budget, such as cost of sales, will rely upon the output from the budgeted activities of the business.

ABB is often used with SMEs as it is relatively straightforward to understand, research and implement. It also links strategic decisions with a plan for the operations of the company. As it focuses on the core activities of the company, ABB is expected to identify and remove any non-value-adding activities.

Zero-based budgeting

Imagine the company had no operating activities, no assets and no staff – this is the approach to take with zero-based budgeting (ZBB). Each time the budget is set, management should assume that the activities of the company are occurring for the first time.

All figures that are entered into the budget are approached using a cost–benefit analysis, so each item of expenditure must be justified to be allowed into the budget. Resources are allocated in the budget based on profitability of their potential activities.

This is a difficult model to perfect. It can also be costly in terms of management time and resources. While ZBB undoubtedly provides the company with an efficient financial forecast, it has been proven to focus on the short term to the detriment of long-term strategy. It is best used if a company is seen to be operating inefficiently and would benefit from a spring clean by taking the attention of management back to the basics of the company.

Rolling budget

This method of budgeting is ideal for young companies or those that are experiencing a period of change, as it constantly reviews the variances of the operating activities.

A continuous rolling budget is prepared initially for 12 months of trading activity – regardless of the planning horizon. Use a standard traditional budgeting template, as the actual format of the budget is not important for the concept to be applied with success. The focus should be on the detail of the first three months of planning. At the end of the first quarter, variance analysis is carried out and the following quarter's figures are updated based on the outcome from the planning or operational variances (Figure 4.6).

Step 1: Create a 12-month budget by month, with the focus on the 1st quarter

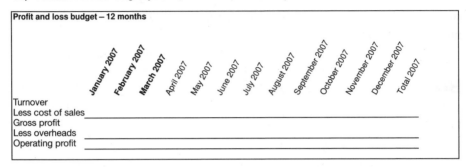

Step 2: At the end of the first quarter, carry out variance analysis and update the second quarter budget

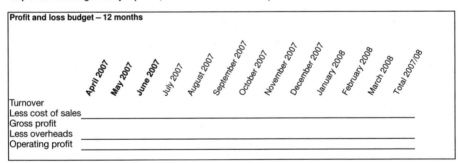

Figure 4.6   Rolling budget process

While the rolling budget has its disadvantages, such as increased management time spent on the continuous budget process, the advantages should outweigh the downside for new, inexperienced companies. It is also said that moving the goal constantly can have an adverse impact on morale of those employees who are looking to achieve the original targets.

Benefits include a higher accountability of management and faster communication of new or altered objectives, making the budget itself more timely and accurate than other methods.

Building the budget

Once a decision has been made on the type of budget that best suits the company, a full budget should be approached by creating smaller budgets for specific business areas, such as sales, cost of sales, labour, overheads and capital expenditure. Once these sub-budgets have been created, they can be consolidated and linked into the main company budget. It's much easier doing it this way as it focuses management's attention on one area at a time. Sometimes details can be missed if we try to look at the big picture, so work on broken-down sections first.

Sales budgeting

A sales budget should provide the expected turnover from each significant customer or customer type. For example, if the company has eight main customers (over 10 per cent or total sales each), a sales forecast should be discussed with each of these customers to gain an understanding of their planned expenditure over the course of the planning horizon. Smaller customer sales, those under 10 per cent of total sales, can be summarised and need not be allocated to a customer. If the company has too many customers for this type of analysis, an assumption of customer expenditure should be made by some other category, such as geography, age or other demographic profile.

The sales budget should also be broken down by product or significant product type. Figure 4.7 gives an example of the format of a monthly sales budget for a company with 5 products and 20 customers in four main geographic zones. The top 12 customers have been identified separately as they each account for more than 5 per cent of total sales. The smaller customers have been grouped together as 'other' in each zone category. The data from the table can be sorted by zone, product or customer sales depending on what type of information is required.

It is important to understand your customer base and its purchasing habits. You will also need to make well-informed assumptions about the demand for your product in the market to ensure a complete and accurate sales budget.

| | Product 1 | | Product 2 | | Product 3 | | Product 4 | | Product 5 | | Total products | |
	Sales (units)	Sales (£)	Sales (units)	Sales (£)	Sales (units)	Sales (£)	Sales (units)	Sales (£)	Sales (units)	Sales (£)	Sales (units)	Sales (£)
Zone 1												
Customer 1												
Customer 2												
Customer 3												
Other												
Total Zone 1												
Zone 2												
Customer 4												
Customer 5												
Customer 6												
Customer 7												
Other												
Total Zone 2												
Zone 3												
Customer 8												
Customer 9												
Customer 10												
Other												
Total Zone 3												
Zone 4												
Customer 11												
Customer 12												
Other												
Total Zone 4												
TOTAL SALES												

Figure 4.7 Sales budget

Chapter 3 provides more detail on the relevance of marketing and accounting in an SME environment.

Material purchases budgeting

The figures included in the material purchases budget should be variable costs only, such as raw materials, components and packaging items that enter the work in progress cycle. If your company does not manufacture a product, the material purchases will be those items that are needed to produce the final unit output for sale, such as branding or accessories.

The materials purchases budget (Figure 4.8) will require the number of units sold in each period, which will drive the materials required. This data is extracted from the sales budget. For example, the sales budget is based on 100 units to be sold in March. The material purchases budget should then calculate what materials are required to make 100 units. This budget should then be used by management to determine when the materials should be ordered and delivered to ensure that 100 units can actually be sold in March.

Labour resource plan

In most small businesses, there are two types of labour – fixed and variable. Fixed costs are those that do not move with the number of units used, made or sold, whereas variable costs are dependent on, and change with, volume and units used, made or sold. The labour resource plan would normally cover only variable labour, which are the employees or contractors whose labour can be directly attributed to the production and/or continuing service of the goods sold by the company.

Variable labour could include those who work in sales or operations such as manufacturing and customer care. Labour should be driven by unit production and included in the overall sales price of a unit.

The labour resource plan feeds off the sales units from the sales budget. The following information will be needed before the labour resource plan can be created:

- levels (skill or grade) of employees;
- rate of hourly and daily pay per level of employees;
- number of hours (or days) required per level per sales unit.

	Product 1		Product 2		Product 3		Product 4		Product 5		Total products	
	Sales (units)	Sales (£)	Sales (units)	Sales (£)	Sales (units)	Sales (£)	Sales (units)	Sales (£)	Sales (units)	Sales (£)	Sales (units)	Sales (£)
Total sales (units)												
Total sales (£)	*information from sales budget*											

Materials required

Material A
Units
price per unit
Material A cost

Material B
Units
price per unit
Material B cost

Material C
Units
price per unit
Material C cost

Total materials
Units
price per unit
Total material cost

Figure 4.8 Materials purchases budget

The following example (Figure 4.9) uses a relatively simplistic model, as it assumes that one sales unit requires three different skill levels of employee and different input rates and pay levels. Example figures have been used for product 1 to indicate how the model is used.

The labour resource plan will tell you how much labour resource is required to produce the budget sales, the cost to the business and the level of skill required to enable efficient resource planning. The above example is based on one month's sales budget and therefore effective labour planning should occur in the month prior to the labour requirement.

The importance of the efficiency of labour resourcing to the profitability of the company is also covered in Chapter 7 on organisational management.

Overheads budgeting

The overheads of a company should be largely fixed, in that they do not fluctuate based on the number of sales unit or unit price. If you notice that an expense item appears to be variable, it could possibly be more accurately accounted for in the materials purchased budget (as a cost of sale) or labour resource plan, depending on its nature.

Overheads include expense items that are incurred when running the operations of the company which support the product or sales-generating activities. These include fixed salaries (such as administration), office expenses (such as printing and stationery), travel and entertainment, and communication costs. The overheads base of a company should be tightly controlled as it can often be a burden to a company that sees its sales fall unexpectedly.

It is important, though, to ensure that overheads are sufficient to support adequately the sales-generating functions of the company. A balance between the two requirements should be determined through the budget process.

Use the output of resource requirements from the sales, material purchase and labour resource budgets as a guide to determine the overheads requirement of the company.

Capital expenditure budget

As with the overheads budget, the capital expenditure budget requirements can be derived from the output of the sales, material purchase and labour resource budgets. For example, if the labour resource plan indicates that five

	Product 1				Product 2				Product 3			
	Sales (units)				Sales (units)				Sales (units)			
Total sales (units)	*information from sales budget* 4											
		Hours	£ / hour	Labour cost		Hours	£ / hour	Labour cost		Hours	£ / hour	Labour cost
Labour type												
Grade 1 - skilled		3	£5.50	£16.50								
Grade 2 - semi-skilled												
Grade 3 - unskilled												
Total labour per sales unit		0.75	£1.38	£4.13								

Product 4				Product 5				Total products			
Sales (units)				Sales (units)				Sales (units)			
	£ / hour	Labour cost		Hours	£ / hour	Labour cost		Hours	£ / hour	Labour cost

Figure 4.9 Labour resource plan

salespeople will be required, three of whom will be operating remotely, it is likely that these three (or perhaps all five) may require a company car. If these cars are to be purchased, they should be factored into a capital expenditure budget. Similarly, if there are to be 20 staff in January increasing to 40 by December, the capital expenditure budget should reflect the requirements – computers, office furniture, sufficient office floor space – of each of these staff members in line with when they will be employed by the company.

The same logic applies to any manufacturing or warehousing. For example, the materials purchases budget indicates that 100 units per day will be produced in July, whereas the existing machinery can produce only 75 units a day. Encountering this scenario during the budgeting process will have three potential outcomes:

- The materials purchased budget must be changed to reflect this bottleneck, which will in turn impact on the sales budget.
- Part of the manufacturing process could be outsourced.
- New equipment should be purchased to cover the bottleneck.

The outcome of this purchase requirement should be factored into the capital expenditure budget.

Consolidate the sub-budgets

Once the sub-budgets have been produced, they should be consolidated into a master budget. Excel is a more than appropriate tool for this exercise, as few SMEs can afford complex management software and often it is not required. If using a spreadsheet, load the sub-budgets into a workbook using one sheet for each, then create a 'face' page, to which the sub-budgets' total will be linked. The 'face' pages of a budget are usually in P&L, balance sheet and cashflow statement format and are the pages which summarise all sub-budget information.

Other budget information to consider

In addition to the planning areas and the sub-budgets covered, the business will be affected by other factors, for which the budget must allow. As we saw in the section on planning, the budget should cover internal and external factors.

I find it useful to use a profit and loss statement and balance sheet as a checklist to ensure that all income and expense items have been captured and are presented on the budget. The financial statements referred to here are as described in detail in Chapter 1.

Internal factors

While most of the internal factors would have been considered in the sub-budgets, the following items should be added to the consolidated budget. Other sources of income generated by the company, outside the normal trading activity, should be treated separately from sales and should not be included in the sales budget.

Other factors include:

- planned investments;
- technology improvements outside normal overheads expenditure;
- equity movements, such as sale of shares or dividends;
- depreciation of fixed assets (if not included in the capital expenditure budget).

External factors

When compiling the budget, remember to look outside your company at the economic environment. Factors such as inflation and interest rates should be considered, as these may impact on the outcome of your financial planning. Further factors to consider include regulatory issues, such as compliance costs specific to the industry, for example health and safety or insurance. Changes in tax rates should also be included, so ensure you have used the latest rates for corporation tax, PAYE taxes and VAT.

Foreign exchange rates fluctuate every day. A budget can use a spot rate (a rate on a particular day) or an average for a fixed period. Most budgets use a spot rate taken at the beginning of the period.

There will be other internal and external factors specific to an individual business, which should be considered by management to complete the budgeting process.

Once the sub-budgets are consolidated, add any other relevant internal or external information to ensure that the final budget is complete. Note – if you're using an application like Excel to link the sub-budgets into the consolidated budget, don't forget to make sure it all adds up! You'd be surprised how many budgets I've seen that don't.

The planning horizon

The term for which a budget is prepared is called the planning horizon. The planning horizon allows a fixed timeframe into the future for which strategies are created and planning, budgets and forecasts are carried out. There are generally two levels to the planning horizon. First, a detailed budget will be carried out for the short term, and second, a more summarised version of the same format budget will be carried out to the predetermined planning horizon. For most established SMEs, the planning horizon is three years – 12 months detailed and the following 2 years in summary.

New businesses could have a shorter planning horizon as they have little or no historic information upon which to base assumptions. In this case a 12-month planning horizon might be more relevant, as anything beyond that would be too speculative. Lenders and financiers, however, are likely to require a three-year planning horizon for any business in which they are looking to invest.

Is there an alternative to formal business planning?

In a word, yes – but tread carefully. It is a brave owner/manager who steers his or her company through the modern business environment without a map as a guide.

Traditional budgeting does have its critics. The use of budgets for effective business planning is not a fool-proof system and can lead to time wasting and over-planning. Managers and staff can become fixated on what the budget says to the detriment of possible opportunities. While budgets are important, it is also essential to maintain an awareness of what is happening outside the budget. Perhaps there will be occasions where going 'off budget' will make the best business sense.

Many SMEs will be relatively new companies with an untried product in an unproven market. Obviously, in cases such as this, planning is much more difficult, as much financial budgeting relies on historic data. The solution is to create alternative scenario planning, such as 'what if' analysis, and to remain as flexible as possible, in terms of management, physical operations and structure of the company.

Another problem with budgeting is that it can promote behaviour which defies goal congruence. For example, if sales managers are remunerated on sales targets, they may be tempted to understate the amount of sales they could make or to overstate the cost of sales if measured on profits. Ensure that the budget is set by an individual who does not directly benefit financially from any measurement against its results.

Freewheeling opportunism

There is a concept referred to as 'freewheeling opportunism', which suggests that a company needn't worry about formal business planning, such as budgets and forecasts. Instead, a business should remain open to opportunities as they arise and be led by market conditions and events.

This type of policy may be difficult to sustain as there is no certainty over whether opportunities will present themselves to the company. Furthermore, if a company has not planned its strategy sufficiently, how can it know which opportunity should become an emergent strategy for the company – will it fit with existing resources and provide the company the return it needs?

There's always an alternative argument, however. Freewheeling opportunism allows a company to be open to opportunities as they arise and be quick to adapt to changes required, which may be needed to take advantage of an opportunity. They are generally more creative and use this as a competitive advantage. What cannot be ignored, though, is that there is a very high level of uncertainty in such a business model and it is not recommended for the majority of small businesses.

Case study

When a client of mine, a financial services company, started up their company, they set their objectives and put together a budget for a three-year planning horizon. The strategy and planning exercise that they carried out proved to be a valuable exercise. The planning research involved investigating what target client companies and individuals wanted and needed from the type of service that they were planning to offer. The directors soon realised that there was a gap in the market for a specific type of corporate finance activity, so they started to develop the idea, which soon grew into the foundation of their budget. Without this strategic planning exercise they would not have chosen to offer a service of such a high level of complexity at such an early stage in the life of the company.

The directors used a combination of a labour resource plan and product-based budget to turn their objectives, ideas and strategy into an operational budget. The labour resource plan was used because their main constraint was the availability of the time of the fee-earning directors. Turnover and profits were limited by the availability of that specific labour resource. The limits of this resource constraint were applied to the planned service, hence the relevance of the product (in this case service) based budget. By using their service as a driver for sales and other associated costs, they could determine the gross profit, which then allowed them to calculate the overhead required to service such a business model. The final output was the projected operating profit.

As a service provider with little asset requirement, profitability was the key information requirement for and from the budget. The directors chose to focus the planning on financial performance in terms of number of clients, minimum value requirement of potential projects and support services required – all key components towards the company's profitability.

This strategic review exercise also raised interesting information about their pricing mechanism, in that there would be a greater demand for their service should their fees be on a contingency basis only, ie they would be paid only on successful completion of a project. As they agreed that one of their objectives was to take market share from the larger investment banks, this high-risk strategy was deemed to be the path to reach their objective. This new pricing mechanism was therefore factored into the budget as it would materially impact on working capital commitments and resource allocation.

The result has been a successful and well-managed company. The directors feel that the company has benefited from the formal planning structure provided by a budget; however, they have retained flexibility as they acknowledge the benefits of remaining flexible in a highly competitive environment.

Conclusion

Planning, strategy and budgets are important to the financial performance of any business. The level of structure of these management tools largely depends on the company and its environment. By choosing the right approach, the planning process will provide management with effective information with which to better manage their company and maximise opportunities that arise throughout its life.

Remember not to lose sight of the company's objectives. Monitor the budgets throughout the planning horizon for which they were created, using them to guide management decisions.

Key points to remember

- Budgeting effectively can result in improved control, efficiency and profitability.
- Company objectives:
  - characteristics of objectives;
  - key strategic objectives include:
    - profitability;
    - return on capital employed (ROCE);
    - dividend policy.
- Strategic and planning review, includes the following environment analysis:
  - PEST analysis – political, economic, social and technological;
  - SWOT analysis – strengths, weaknesses, opportunities and threats;
  - gap analysis – compare objectives with expected performance;
  - Porter's five competitive forces analysis – used in periods of change or instability, this method approaches the environment in a defensive manner.
- Different types of budget:
  - traditional budgeting;
  - incremental budgeting;
  - profit-motive-based budgeting;
  - activity-based budgeting;
  - zero-based budgeting;
  - rolling budget.

■ Build the budget, by creating the following sub-budgets:
  – sales budget;
  – materials purchases budget;
  – labour resource plan;
  – overheads budget;
  – capital expenditure budget.
■ The planning horizon – what timeframe is suitable for planning your business?
■ Freewheeling opportunism – an alternative to formal budgeting.

Decision making

As we have seen in the previous chapters, management accounting and performance management techniques can be used by small businesses to improve efficiency and financial performance. It's not all about accounting, however, as better legal, marketing and organisational management can also impact directly on profits. These areas all tie back into management accounting as profit is the objective for most companies and thus accounting will play a key role in any function that is designed to improve a company's profitability.

While there are many other aspects to the successful management of resources, quantitative analysis is a key component of management accounting techniques. Quantitative analysis, in this context, simply means reviewing the performance of the business using data-driven financial models. It may sound complex; however, its application can be kept simple for the SME.

This chapter will focus on useful decision-making tools used by management accountants. These tools have been adapted to be not only suitable but highly beneficial to a small, private company.

Work through the different decision-making tools and determine which of them would benefit and be appropriate for your specific business operations. The following applications are relatively generic, in that they should apply to all small businesses, and their value can be seen on day-to-day decisions just as with one-off management decisions. Appropriate use of these tools can make a positive impact on your business and its operations.

Management accounting terminology

Before looking at each method in detail, there are some management accounting terms that are frequently used in quantitative analysis and therefore the user of management accounting techniques should be aware of these as they are common vernacular in decision-making and performance analysis tools that may be encountered:

- **Avoidable costs** – specific costs of an activity which could only have been avoided if that activity did not exist.
- **Committed costs** – costs that have been promised, but not yet paid, are also generally omitted from management decision making.
- **Cost driver** – a factor to which the change in cost of an activity can be attributed. Often used as the basis for analysis of a specific cost or activity such as a production unit.
- **Notional costs** – a representational cost figure used for the decision-making processes which reflects a cost that should have actually been incurred but was not and therefore must be represented with a notional cost.
- **Opportunity costs** – the value of the benefit which is foregone by taking one course of action over the other. There is no requirement for a physical payment to occur, as foregoing income or payment is sufficient to be classed as an opportunity cost.
- **Relevant costs** – these are costs which are appropriate to management decision making and will therefore be included in any analysis. Relevant costs should be future, not past or sunk, costs.
- **Sunk costs** – costs that have already been incurred, which should not factor into analysis for decision making.
- **Throughput contribution** – sales revenue less direct material costs.

Management accounting techniques

There are many management accounting tools used for quantitative analysis. This chapter will provide a description and practical example of the four methods of analysis that are deemed the most appropriate to the small business environment.

The methods that will be reviewed in more detail are:

1. decision trees;
2 variance analysis;
3. cashflow analysis;
4. Pareto analysis.

These methods are all relatively simple management theories to understand and apply to a working business.

Decision trees

A decision tree is a pictorial representation of a sequential series of decisions and their expected outcomes, which are quantified to allow comparison with other courses of action. Decision trees work on the basis of probability analysis, and allow for relatively complicated probability questions to be answered. Probability analysis simply reports on the likelihood of specific events based on the financial data collected.

Decision trees are incredibly useful for small businesses as they allow management to review and compare the options available, yet they do not require sophisticated analysis programs to produce. They are well suited to address the typical problems of a small business operating in a challenging environment.

The tree format allows management to view a clear, concise, quantified picture of the expected outcomes of the available options, which should allow for accurate decision making to best benefit the company. Each branch of the tree will reflect the expected value of a particular course of action, so each option is comparable against its alternatives.

There are three stages to using decision tree analysis. The first is to collect all relevant raw data, the second step is to construct the tree, and the third is to analyse the expected outcomes to provide the decision required.

Collect raw data for the decision tree

The output of the decision tree will be only as accurate as the raw data used as inputs. It is important that the raw data captured has integrity in that it is accurate, timely, relevant and quantifiable.

The raw data required for the tree will depend on the nature of the decision to be made, so it is practical to start with this as the initial data collection point. Once the objective and the decision to be made have been identified, determine the detail of the alternative options that are available, thus creating the need to make a decision. It may be that the best alternative is to do nothing – this is fine provided alternative scenarios have been investigated in full.

Relevant data can now be collected, such as costs or sales pricing or marketing statistics. Ensure that all data available is collected and entered into a format that can be used in the analysis to ensure accuracy of the basis for the decision. When collecting the data it is important to reflect all possible options and their levels of risk and uncertainty. The options must also be quantified to enable the analysis.

Construct the decision tree

It is standard practice to draw the decision tree from left to right in a portrait view, using a square for the decision points, lines for the options and a circle for each outcome point. The tree should also appear in chronological order from left to right, thus displaying the sequence of events as decisions are required. The practical example below will give further detail on how the decision tree should be constructed.

Analyse the expected outcomes

Each branch will lead to two or more expected values, based on the options available. The probability figure stated as the output from the tree should be used as the basis of this calculation. The manager should then compare the expected values from the tree to calculate the value of each decision, thus indicating when company resources will be best employed.

Decision tree – practical example

Shoe Ltd is a shoe manufacturer and retailer. It has £100,000 cash available to use as an investment into three potential new product lines, each with different levels of price, profitability and sales volumes. Market research has also been conducted to estimate customer take-up on each type of shoe.

Each shoe requires an initial investment of £50,000, so the director is faced with a decision to choose two out of three options.

The three new shoe products have been named Coo, Boo and Foo. The Coo has been estimated as having a 90 per cent take-up from customers as it is a variation on an existing model which has been very successful. The Boo has a take-up estimate of 85 per cent; however, the Foo has been estimated at only 55 per cent as it is a new design that has been targeted to divert away from market trends as a signature item.

Shoe Ltd's marketing department have given the unit sales estimations along with the sales price set for each new product. The finance department has provided the cost estimates of each new shoe to complete the unit profit analysis.

This data has been summarised in Table 5.1.

Table 5.1   Decision tree data (Shoe Ltd)

Product	Take-up	Units	Sales	Cost	Profits
Coo	90%	10,000	£395,000	£158,000	£237,000
Boo	85%	10,000	£445,000	£190,000	£255,000
Foo	55%	7,500	£595,000	£190,000	£405,000

Another option for the director is that he retains the £100,000 for alternative investment and does not deliver any new products to market. While this is a genuine financial option, non-financial consequences should be considered, such as perception of the brand. It could be seen as lack of innovativeness if no new product is delivered to market. The decision tree should then be constructed as shown in Figure 5.1.

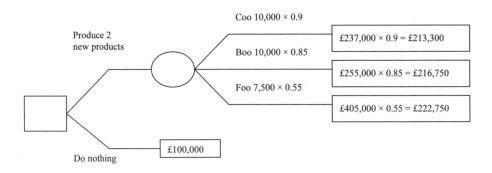

Figure 5.1   Decision tree (Shoe Ltd)

The output from the decision tree indicates that Foo is the most profitable per unit, and is estimated to have sufficient take-up to match the overall contribution from Coo and Boo. The financial analysis indicates that the working capital of £100,000 available should then be allocated to investing in Foo and Boo.

Variance analysis

Variance analysis is a very simple tool used by managers to identify performance. This type of analysis could be applied to sales, profits, overheads – any area of financial performance can be analysed by comparing actual performance with budgeted performance. Variance analysis can also compare actual performance against the company's forecast and competitors' or market figures.

Variance analysis is designed to identify management areas of weakness or poor control within the operations of the company. It can also identify areas of planning weaknesses. It will not, however, provide the outcome or a direction for change, as it will merely highlight areas that require further management attention. While this, in itself, is an important management tool for decision making, variance analysis would normally be used in conjunction with other decision-making techniques.

We look at basic variance analysis as part of the management accounting pack (MAP) in Chapter 6, and while variance at profit and loss statement level is important, it can also be useful for management decision making to drill down into further detail on financial areas of key importance to the business. It is useful to use variance analysis to determine the difference between operating and planning variances. For example, if sales were reported at 10 per cent less than planned, the variance analysis should tell management whether this was due to genuine poor sales or inadequate planning. This is a step further than traditional variance analysis which implies that any variance is due to performance issues only.

The following practical example will show the importance of identifying the difference between an operational and a planning variance.

Bag Ltd's budget for March is to produce and sell 1,000 new design bags at £100 each. The cost of sale (variable cost) for each item is £50.

Budget	£
Sales (1,000 units)	100,000
Cost of sales	(50,000)
Gross profit	50,000
Overheads	(30,000)
Operating profit	20,000

During February, it became known to management that there would be a distribution problem and it was estimated that the new design bags would not arrive at Bag Ltd's retail stores until 15 March, thereby giving only half the sales volumes that were originally budgeted. A revised forecast for March was then drawn up as follows:

Forecast	£
Sales (500 units)	50,000
Cost of sales	(25,000)
Gross profit	25,000
Overheads	(30,000)
Operating loss	(5,000)

Remember that cost of sales is variable costs and therefore are incurred only with each unit of production. Overheads, however, are assumed to be fixed and therefore will be incurred, and paid, regardless of sales or production volume.

In April, the actual figures for March were reported as follows:

Actual	£
Sales (600 units)	60,000
Cost of sales	(30,000)
Gross profit	30,000
Overheads	(30,000)
Operating profit	NIL

While we can see that the total operating profit variance against budget was £20,000, it would be useful for management to determine just how much of that variance was due to poor planning and how much was due to normal operational factors. This analysis is carried out using the following planning and operational variances.

Planning variance

The planning variance is designed to compare the revised forecast with the original budget.

Revised forecast sales volume (units)	500	
Less Original budgeted sales volume (units)	1,000	
Total planning variance (units)	500	(Adverse)
× standard gross profit per unit	£50	
Planning variance	£25,000	(Adverse)

Operational variance

The operational variance is calculated in the normal way; however, it compares the actual units sold with the revised forecast units:

Actual sales volume (units)	600	
Less Revised forecast sales volume (units)	500	
Total planning variance (units)	100	(Favourable)
× standard gross profit per unit	£50	
Planning variance	£5,000	(Favourable)

So, if management were to look merely at the total overall variance, they would know that operating profits showed an adverse variance of £20,000. Through this effective analysis technique, management have the additional information that March showed a £25,000 adverse variance due to the planning issue, whereas operationally, they performed with a £5,000 favourable variance. This allows management to focus attention on preventing future planning issues, knowing that operationally they are performing in line with budget.

Cashflow analysis

Cashflow is often the real basis for management decision making. Regardless of the outcome of other models, decisions will be made based on how much cash or liquid assets one decision will provide over another.

The approach to cashflow analysis is simple. Compare how much cash is available against how much cash is needed for a certain project, business activity or investment. The value of cash made from a project or investment is then calculated and compared with other available options. This general type of analysis can be applied to any area of business where cash is required.

It is important to remember that cashflow analysis is concerned only with cash inflows and outflows – profits are rarely factored into the calculation. In Chapter 2 on working capital, we discussed the importance of the distinction between cash and profits – this concept is also relevant to cashflow analysis.

The two main forms of cashflow analysis used in business are net present value (NPV) and internal rate of return (IRR).

Net present value (NPV)

The net present value of cash is the value of cash inflows that are earned from future returns or outflows required for future commitments as stated in the current value of money. For example, management are faced with a decision between two investment opportunities. The first would provide a £100 return on an investment in two years' time against the second investment, which would return £120 in three years' time. To make the decision, the figures would have to be comparable, and therefore should both be translated into current values.

Calculating an NPV of future cashflows is very simple. The only data requirements are the cashflows required for the project and the cost of capital. The cost of capital should be the cost of debt or equity or a weighted average cost of the two if both are employed in the business. See Chapter 12 for a full description of how to calculate a weighted average cost of capital.

Let's look at the following example to see how an NPV calculation can help management make business decisions.

Land Ltd has the option to invest in a land development project over the next three years. Managers must decide whether or not the project will provide a sufficient return for the company. The cost of capital to the company is 10 per cent and the company can gain 5 per cent return for cash on deposit at the bank, so any return from the project must be significantly higher than this to account for the level of risk involved. The estimated cashflows for the project are as follows:

Year 0	(£10,000)	cash outflow
Year 1	£10,000	cash inflow
Year 2	£12,500	cash inflow
Year 3	£15,000	cash inflow

Once the cash inflow and outflow figures have been identified, simply apply the cost of capital percentage as the discount factor to the cashflow figures. This will provide a present value of cashflows for each year, which, when totalled, will provide a total net present value for the project. Land Ltd's NPV for the project would be calculated as shown in Table 5.2.

Table 5.2 Net present value (Land Ltd)

	Cashflow	**Discount factor: 10%**		**NPV**
Year 0	(£35,000)	1.000		(£35,000)
Year 1	£10,000	$1/1.1$	0.909	£9,091
Year 2	£20,000	$1/1.1^2$	0.826	£16,529
Year 3	£30,000	$1/1.1^3$	0.751	£22,539
				£13,159

The NPV of £13,159 should now be compared with any other investment opportunities that may be available to Land Ltd to ensure its capital is best employed to maximise shareholder wealth.

Maximising shareholder wealth may not be simply a matter of achieving increased short-term profits. Directors must consider a range of factors to ensure that the right management decisions are being made to increase the value of shareholders' equity. This may mean fewer profits in the short term for greater overall profits. Any decision made should tie in with corporate objectives (as covered in Chapter 4). Chapter 11 has further information on the motive of shareholders and the obligations of the directors to meet their required return on investment.

Note that an NPV calculation should always commence with year 0, which is the current starting point of the analysis, with year 1 starting after the first full year of the project.

Internal rate of return (IRR)

The internal rate of return (IRR) of discounted cashflows gives a yield from a project or investment, in which capital is employed, in a percentage format. This percentage can then be compared with other projects or investment opportunities that may be available to the company.

The formula to apply to the IRR calculation is:

$$IRR = A + \left(\frac{P}{P + N} \times (B - A) \right) \%$$

Where:

A is the rate of return with a positive NPV
B is the rate of return with a negative NPV
P is the amount of positive NPV
N is the absolute value of the negative NPV.

To start with, two NPV calculations must be carried out. Use the method given in the NPV section above as the formula. The two discount factors used will be to provide information for the formula only – they will not form any other part of the decision-making process and do not need to be based on any figure from the business. As the formula requires a positive NPV and a negative NPV, the two discount factors should be chosen to provide this data.

We'll use the same details from the example of Land Ltd as used in the above NPV calculation; therefore the actual discount factor is 10 per cent. We need to obtain one positive NPV and one negative NPV, so guess at two percentages that will provide that outcome, such as 12 and 30 per cent. Again, these two percentages are not based on any information from the business, they are chosen at random, simply to provide the inputs required for the IRR formula.

Table 5.3 Internal rate of return calculation (Land Ltd)

	Cashflow	Discount factor: 12%		NPV
Year 0	(£35,000)		1.000	(£35,000)
Year 1	£10,000	1 / 1.12	0.893	£8,929
Year 2	£20,000	1 / 1.12²	0.797	£15,944
Year 3	£30,000	1 / 1.12³	0.712	£21,353
				£11,226

	Cashflow	Discount factor: 30%		NPV
Year 0	(£35,000)		1.000	(£35,000)
Year 1	£10,000	1 / 1.3	0.769	£7,692
Year 2	£20,000	1 / 1.3²	0.592	£11,834
Year 3	£30,000	1 / 1.3³	0.455	£13,655
				(£1,818)

Table 5.3 provides details of the two NPV percentages chosen at random and their NPV values.

Now, apply the IRR formula with the figures from the above NPV calculation factored in:

$$IRR = 12 + \left(\frac{11{,}226}{11{,}226 + 1{,}818} \times (30{-}12) \right) \%$$

$$IRR = 27.5\%$$

The internal rate of return for the project for Land Ltd is 27.5 per cent. This should be compared with its normal expected IRR from projects and investment. This comparison is the basis of decision making for management.

Discounted cashflow (DCF)

Using the discounted cashflow analysis (DCF) is a very useful technique for decision making. The DCF formula is explained in detail in Chapter 12, where it is applied to a company valuation. It is equally useful for investment appraisal or other business decisions that require a decision on capital employment.

Pareto analysis

Pareto analysis is a simple management accounting tool designed to focus management attention on areas of the company that contribute real value. This real value may be in terms of sales, profits, efficiency of overheads or the labour resource.

The economist Vilfredo Pareto found that 80 per cent of a nation's wealth was represented by just 20 per cent of its population. This theory has subsequently been applied to business, resulting in the '80/20 rule'. The concept of the 80/20 rule can be applied to many areas of the business to aid management prioritise where they should allocate their focus and the resources of the company in order to maximise profits.

Applications of Pareto analysis, or the 80/20 rule, for the small business can include the following common assumptions: 20 per cent of customers provide 80 per cent of profits and 20 per cent of products contribute 80 per cent of sales. The analyst should not expect a clear 80/20, as the model argues the basic principle that a small number of products often yield a high proportion of income and on this basis, management should focus their attention accordingly.

Example of Pareto analysis – P Ltd

Using the example of the customers and profits, Pareto analysis should be carried out by management to assess the level of customer power within P Ltd. Table 5.4 shows the raw data provided by accounts on sales and profits as generated by the company's 10 customers.

Once the raw data is received it will need to be sorted, in descending order, and arranged into the Pareto analysis format:

Table 5.4   Raw data for Pareto analysis (P Ltd)

Customer	Turnover	Profits
1	1,000	300
2	1,500	700
3	2,000	550
4	1,050	400
5	5,070	1,000
6	7,394	2,500
7	5,045	1,000
8	4,560	2,000
9	1,000	650
10	750	350
	29,369	9,450

Step 1   Separate the two pieces of information – sales and profits – as these will be analysed separately before being compared in the final analysis.

Step 2   Rank the customers in descending order of sales value.

Step 3   Calculate the total percentage of each customer's sales value in relation to the total sales figure.

Step 4   Calculate the cumulative sales figure, from the top-ranking customer down to the smallest customer.

Step 5   Calculate the cumulative percentage figure, from the top ranking customer to the smallest customer.

Step 6   Repeat steps 1 to 5 with the profit data.

The final Pareto analysis table should be represented as shown in Table 5.5.

Management should use the information from this table to identify that 77.7 per cent of sales come from just four customers. This is a threat to the company and steps should be taken to avoid reliance on so few customers. The profits provide a similar picture of reliance on key customers, although slightly less so, as only 68.8 per cent of profits are generated by the top four customers. Interestingly, customer 5 is ranked 2 for sales, but only 4 for profitability, while customer 8 is ranked 4 for sales and 2 for profitability. This should be investigated, as it could be an error in data or a genuine difference

Table 5.5 Pareto analysis – customers (P Ltd)

Customer	Sales	% of Sales	Cum sales	Cum %	Customer	Profits	% of Profits	Cum profits	Cum %
6	7,394	23.9	7,394	23.9	6	2,500	26.5	2,500	26.5
5	6,070	19.6	13,464	43.6	8	2,000	21.2	4,500	47.6
7	5,570	18.0	19,034	61.6	7	1,000	10.6	5,500	58.2
8	4,980	16.1	24,014	77.7	5	1,000	10.6	6,500	68.8
3	1,760	5.7	25,774	83.4	2	700	7.4	7,200	76.2
2	1,500	4.9	27,274	88.3	9	650	6.9	7,850	83.1
4	1,050	3.4	28,324	91.7	3	550	5.8	8,400	88.9
9	970	3.1	29,294	94.8	4	400	4.2	8,800	93.1
1	860	2.8	30,154	97.6	10	350	3.7	9,150	96.8
10	750	2.4	30,904	100.0	1	300	3.2	9,450	100.0
	30,904					9,450			

in profitability levels per customer. As profitability is likely to be an objective of the company, management should investigate why customer 8 is more profitable and try to replicate this reason, should it be genuine, against other customers.

Pareto analysis is designed to provide management with a better understanding of the operations of a company. It is also a useful tool for control over customer power, as seen in the above example, for stock control and control of overheads and variable costs.

While it is a useful tool, its output should be considered along with other decision-making methods, as Pareto analysis alone does not address all aspects of a business situation.

Case study

AdCo is a subsidiary company of a multinational corporation. While technically being part of a large group, AdCo operated as a stand-alone entity and management were expected to make decisions as though they were the owners of the business, so for management accounting purposes we can treat them as a small business. The directors operated without any form of financial analysis or decision-making tools for three years, before they took steps to try to better understand their business and its performance. It was suggested that they adopt variance analysis and Pareto analysis as part of their management accounting information. Variance analysis was used against budgets set by the parent company, so it was essential that management understood why performance was not meeting certain areas of the budget.

Management began to have the tools to answer why the business was underperforming against expectations from the parent company. It turned out that the budget did not take certain unique environmental factors of the UK market into consideration, such as labour costs and debtor behaviour. Once the managers of AdCo could identify the adversely performing areas, they could rectify the problems of poor budgeting combined with poor performance in certain areas of operations.

Pareto analysis was introduced to underline the strength certain customers had over their business. Two customers equated to over 80 per cent of turnover. While this had been generally assumed, it took the clarity of a Pareto analysis chart to understand the threat this brought to their business. Management took appropriate steps by introducing new customers to dilute the control.

Conclusion

There are many management accounting and quantitative techniques available to small business managers which can improve the performance of the company. Each of the methods explained in this chapter can be used for many functions within a company and should be used by management in the normal course of business but more specifically when important decisions are required to be made.

Key points to remember

- Decision making relies on the use of quantitative analysis as a key management accounting tool. Quantitative analysis is the use of data-driven financial models to derive information to use as the basis of management decisions.
- Management accounting terminology relevant to decision-making tools includes:
  - avoidable costs;
  - committed costs;
  - cost driver;
  - notional costs;
  - opportunity costs;
  - relevant costs;
  - sunk costs;
  - throughput contribution.
- Decision-making tools relevant to SMEs include:
  - Decision trees – pictorial representation of a sequence of decisions and their expected value outputs.

- Variance analysis – comparison of actual and expected performance.
- Cashflow analysis – review of cash inflows and outflows to manage the liquidity of the company. Net present value of cash is used to make investment decisions.
- Pareto analysis – 80/20 rule used by management for resource allocation and avoidance of risk exposure.

2

Business management and operations

6

Management accounting pack (MAP)

Many businesses prepare basic financial information such as a profit and loss statement, a balance sheet and a cashflow statement, and rely purely on these to manage and develop a business. They are not enough. To manage a business successfully, a manager must look at historic, current and future information regarding not only their own company, but also the environment in which the company operates.

Financial information will provide an idea of how the business is performing, but it will not provide all the tools for planning, analysis and decision making.

When I visit a new SME client, the first thing I do is ask to see what information they use in management meetings – those who actually have management meetings, that is. More often than not, I am given a set of financial statements as described above. It is rare to find a small business that will go beyond historic financial information to plan the future of their operational and financial success.

So, what should be in a 'management accounting pack' (MAP), and how, when and by whom should it be used?

Case study

At the first meeting I had with Bath Co, it was clear they needed to have better control over the future of their business. There was no management accounting information and as such they couldn't forecast accurately, which was causing the directors a great deal of stress. The solution was to introduce solid financial information based on data which was already being captured at operational level. This information was then fed into a MAP tailored for their business, to inform the directors of their most profitable product, how to make the most profit from their existing resources and how much working capital was needed in 12 months to expand in line with their plans. This MAP also gave peace of mind that there was enough stock on hand to meet short-term future orders. The directors of Bath Co now appreciate the need for a MAP for forward planning.

Before we look at the contents of a typical MAP, some time should be spent thinking about the following questions.

Who will be using this report?

Will the shareholders want to view a MAP as well as business managers? Perhaps the owners of the business would like to invite any important stakeholder, such as the bank or significant investor, along to a management meeting where the MAP will be the central document under discussion. Will more junior staff be using the MAP? If so, certain language and particularly sensitive information should be treated accordingly. The contents of the MAP should be at an appropriate level for the range of users.

Table 6.1 suggests some of the uses that specific stakeholders or report users may have. Chapter 1 describes each main stakeholder of a small business and their general objectives.

Table 6.1 Map uses and users

Report user	Internal or external	Uses for the MAP
Shareholder	Internal	To assess the value of the company and the potential return on investment at any one time. They may also want to ensure that the assets of the company are being used efficiently to maximise profits, which are ultimately owned by the shareholders.
Employee	Internal	Communication with employees of a company is critical, though often a MAP will contain financially sensitive information and its distribution should be limited. Employees, however, deserve to know what is going on in the company and motivation will be improved. Prepare a clear, concise report of the overall performance of the company so that employees know that their time is being well spent.
Department managers	Internal	Often department managers focus on their core business and don't get a chance to look at other areas of the business during the month. The presentation of the MAP will enable them to see the company as a whole and how efficiently their department contributes to the overall performance of the business.
Bank or other lender	External	Lenders will want to see profitability and solvency as two of the main financial indicators to ensure that repayment of their loan will continue. They will often need to see a forecast for at least 12 months as part of their requirement from the MAP.
Board directors	Internal	The board will be interested in an overall picture of how the company is performing, especially if they are non-executive directors, meaning that they do not work with the company on a day-to-day basis. Directors should be interested in summary-level information covering the key areas of the business.

How often will the report be produced?

Generally, monthly production of the MAP is sufficient. More time will go into producing a MAP than a normal set of accounts, so keep in mind the opportunity cost of the resource of the person(s) who will be spending valuable time preparing the report. Most well-designed MAPs should be automated from the source data, thereby reducing the level of staff input time required for the task. If a business is undergoing a period of change or instability, a fortnightly or even weekly review of the MAP (or extract) might be more appropriate.

What are the needs of the parties who will review the map?

Different people will want to focus on different information. A shareholder may be interested in levels of retained profits, whereas a sales manager will want information about sales levels against targets. While it's true that you can't keep everyone happy all of the time, a MAP must try to satisfy all requirements without becoming too focused on any one area. This is always a tricky thing to do, and the MAP will inevitably be a work in progress (WIP) until all parties are satisfied with the information content. We will focus on this in greater detail later in Chapter 9 on information systems.

What factors are important to the business?

The MAP must be concise, so it must immediately address the root of the important issues and objectives of the company. For example, if product profitability is key, which it most often is, then a statement should be created on how profitable certain products are against another (as covered in Chapter 3) upon which resource allocation decisions can be made. Where a company is asset heavy, a metric on how efficient the assets are performing towards achieving profitability might be relevant. If the company has a high labour cost, it might be useful to assess where each labour unit is working and how profitable they are. All of these performance metrics will be covered in greater detail in later chapters, but this gives you an idea of how to approach the MAP. The easiest way is to take the three largest costs in the company and analyse them against profits.

Once these and other key questions have been answered, a bespoke MAP can be created for the company.

Contents of a MAP

The contents of a typical MAP should include the following:

1. profit and loss statement (P&L) – reports the income, expenditure and profits achieved during a specific period;
2. balance sheet – a snapshot of the business assets, liabilities and equity as at a specific date, normally at the end of the reporting period of the corresponding P&L;
3. cashflow statement – detail of cash inflows and outflows during a specific period, with opening and closing cash balances;
4. product profitability statement – an analysis of profit by product which should include all relevant resources and their associated costs;
5. key performance indicators – includes performance measures and an analysis of the areas which hold particular importance for the company;
6. other information relevant to the business – this may be financial or non-financial and should include any relevant information not covered in the above-mentioned reports.

You will notice that the MAP starts with the three basic financial statements that most companies already use – P&L, balance sheet and cashflow statement. This is what business managers want, need and expect to see at the front of any MAP. The other reports analyse historic data to provide tools for decision making about the future of the business and should be tailored to the specific operations and information needs of the business.

Now, let's look at each of these reporting areas in turn.

Note that, for the purposes of this book and therefore level of financial report described, we assume a single entity company. Accounts reported will therefore not require consolidation, which takes a different format.

Profit and loss statement (P&L)

A P&L is a measure of financial performance for a fixed period. It is customary to produce figures on a monthly and year to date (cumulative) basis, unless otherwise specified.

The format of a profit and loss statement should meet the needs of the internal accounting function in addition to the statutory reporting requirements of the report. I would always recommend the P&L be set up using the statutory format as the template. This ensures that the company captures the necessary information and also negates the requirement to restate the reporting for year-end purposes.

The statutory P&L format is shown in Table 6.2.

Table 6.2   Profit and loss statement – statutory format

Profit and loss statement for the period January 2007

	January 2007	Year to date
	£	£
Turnover	x	x
Cost of sales	(x)	(x)
Gross profit/(loss)	x	**x**
Distribution costs	(x)	(x)
Overheads	(x)	(x)
	x	x
Other operating income	x	x
Income from shares and investments	x	x
Amounts written off investments	(x)	(x)
Interest payable and similar charges	(x)	(x)
Profit/(loss) on ordinary activities before tax	x	x
Corporation tax	(x)	(x)
Profit/(loss) on ordinary activities after tax	x	x
Extraordinary profit/(loss)	x	x
Tax on extraordinary profit/(loss)	(x)	(x)
Profit/(loss) for the financial year	x	x

While this report may look complicated, with a lot of information that may not be needed on an operational or managerial basis, it is important to set up the P&L in this format initially. From this format, extract an operating P&L, which will be the format used in the MAP. This simply takes the top

Table 6.3   Profit and loss statement – operating format

Profit and loss statement (operating) for the period January 2007				
	January 2007 £		Year to date £	
Turnover		x		x
Cost of sales				
Purchases	x		x	
Changes in stock	x		x	
Total cost of sales		(x)		(x)
Gross profit/(loss)		x		x
Distribution costs				
Carriage	x		x	
Warehousing	x		x	
Packaging	x		x	
Total distribution costs		(x)		(x)
Overheads				
Staff salaries & wages	x		x	
Hire costs	x		x	
Office expenses	x		x	
Professional fees	x		x	
Total overheads		(x)		(x)
Profit/(loss) on ordinary activities before tax		x		x
Corporation tax		(x)		(x)
Profit/(loss) on ordinary activities after tax		x		x

section of the statutory format P&L and delves into more detail on some of the operating lines.

An example of a P&L used in a MAP would be presented as shown in Table 6.3.

As you can see, the second format, the operating P&L, is more detailed and can be tailored to the business and its operations. If there is no stock, take out the stock movement line in the cost of sales; however, if there is stock, most readers of the accounts will want to see the stock movement stated clearly on the face (front page) of the P&L.

This format is a guide. Adapt it to your business needs and the requirements of those using the MAP.

The face of the P&L should not be any more detailed than the operational format given above. Should any further breakdown of P&L items be required, they should be included on supporting pages. Examples of further analysis to P&L items include:

- sales – by geographical or other type of analysis;
- purchases – by product or product type, such as specific components;
- changes in stock – by type of stock;
- distribution – by warehouse site, distribution format (air, land, sea);
- overheads – by staff location or grade level, analysis of overheads spend by department, bank charges split by normal and debt financing.

As you can see, there are many further ways to break down P&L items. Again, tailor these to the company and what is actually deemed to be useful information by those using the MAP. Generally, there is little use analysing an item that is not material to the overall operating position. As a rule of thumb, anything under 5 per cent of turnover need not be analysed further unless there is a reason for doing so.

Balance sheet

The balance sheet is a measure of the financial position of the company at any given date. It is customary to produce a balance sheet at the end of the reporting period, normally monthly, and certainly at the end of the company's financial year.

A typical balance sheet format reads as shown in Table 6.4. Note that the 'total assets less liabilities' figure should equal the 'total capital and reserves' figure exactly, hence providing a balance sheet.

Some of these balance sheet accounts need further explanation, so let's look at each of those in turn.

Fixed assets

The fixed assets should include a note on the cost of the assets and how much has been posted to the P&L as depreciation during the life of the assets. The

Table 6.4   Balance sheet format

Balance sheet as at 31 January 2007		
	£	£
Fixed assets		x
Current assets		
Stock	x	
Trade debtors	x	
Cash at bank	x	
Other current assets	x̲	
Total current assets		x
Current liabilities		
Trade creditors	(x)	
Bank loans	(x)	
Other creditors	(x)	
Total current liabilities		(x̲)
Total net current assets		x
Creditors falling due after one year		(x̲)
Total assets less liabilities		x̲
Capital and Reserves		
Share capital		x
Profit and loss account b/f		x
Reserves		x̲
Total capital and reserves		x̲

cost less accumulated depreciation balance is the net book value (NBV) of the asset, which is the amount stated on the face (front page) of the balance sheet. More detail, if required, can be provided as a note on a separate schedule behind the face page. The fixed assets section should include intangible items (eg development costs), tangible items (eg furniture, buildings) and investments (eg shares in and loans to other parties).

The fixed asset note format is as follows:

Fixed assets – computer	£
Cost	x
Accumulated depreciation	(x)
Net book value	x

Current assets

Stock should reflect the value of the physical stock at the end of the period, including raw materials, WIP and finished goods. Stock should always be stated at the lower of cost and net realisable value (ie what it can realistically be sold for in the current market).

Trade debtors should be the total amount due from 'trade' debtors only, ie monies due in from customers. This figure should include only amounts due from debtors that were incurred during the course of providing goods to a customer. All other amounts due from activities outside normal trading should be treated separately, normally as 'other debtors'.

Cash at bank should be the bank statement balance after all adjustments for unpresented payments and receipts have been made. Assume that all cheques written have been presented and all bank transfers have cleared – this is the 'cash book balance', which is used on the balance sheet to reflect the cash at bank.

Other debtors may include prepayments and accrued income.

Current liabilities

The word 'current', in the context of the balance sheet, means due and payable within the next 12 months. Only include items which fall due within this period.

As with trade debtors, trade creditors should include only those creditors who occur in the normal course of business and appear on the aged creditor listing. Any entity to which money is owed through non-core business activities should appear in other creditors rather than trade creditors.

Bank loans should state the actual amount owed, which is calculated by deducting interest and repayments made and adding on any additional charges to the original capital borrowed. Other creditors should include accruals, taxation or any other creditor balances which are owed by or relevant to the company within the next 12 months only.

Creditors falling due after 12 months should be listed separately under the relevant line on the balance sheet, after the net current assets total.

Capital and reserves

Share capital is the amount of shares that the company has issued. This is the initial and subsequent equity of the company as raised through share capital.

Profit and loss balances from previous years are brought forward on to each balance sheet to provide a cumulative balance of the company's profitability to date. Some companies like to list out the years on the balance sheet, but one cumulative total is normally sufficient.

The reserves section should include all reserve amounts, the most common of which are balances from the revaluation of an asset.

Cashflow statement

A cashflow statement is a report of cash inflows and outflows and is a measure of liquidity. We covered the complexities of cashflow in Chapter 2 on working capital, so we will now look at the format of the cashflow statement as part of the MAP (Table 6.5).

Keeping the cashflow in an operating format enables management to understand how much working capital is being spent on core operating activities. While I stressed in Chapter 2 the importance of understanding that cash does not necessarily equal profit, it is convenient to keep the cashflow statement in a format as close to the P&L as possible to facilitate understanding and comparison.

Product profitability statement

Every business should carry out profitability calculations on their product set. It is essential to know the unit profit of each product that is being sold to the market. The two main reasons for this information to be generated are: 1) marketing – to set a sales price that will generate a profit; and 2) operations – to ensure that company resources are being used effectively by producing the most profitable product for which there is sufficient demand.

These factors lie at the core of the financial stability of the business and should be monitored and analysed as a priority in any MAP. The statement

Table 6.5   Cashflow statement

Cashflow statement for the period January 2007	£
Cash inflows	
Sales	x
Other operating activities	x
Total operating cash inflows	**x**
Cash outflows	
Cost of sales	(x)
Overheads	(x)
Total operating cash outflows	**(x)**
Other cashflows	
Interest income	x
Interest payments	(x)
Taxation	x/(x)
Capital expenditure	x
Acquisitions and disposals	x/(x)
Servicing of debt finance	(x)
Total other cashflows	**(x)**
Total net cash movement for the month	**x**
Opening cash balance	(x)
Closing cash balance	**(x)**

shown in Table 6.6 is a suggested format for the presentation of a product profitability statement in the MAP; however, as each company will have different data inputs and information outputs, as well as levels of complexity, the final presentation can be modified to consider the factors bespoke to the business.

Before we look at an example, the concept of overhead absorption should be explained briefly. Overhead absorption is the level of overheads to be absorbed by the profits generated by a specific product or activity. This concept is explained in the example in Table 6.6. The key impact on company financial performance of producing one unit will be its contribution to overheads. We describe product contribution as being the sales price less all variable costs, giving the profit. This profit is then 'contributing' to the overhead (fixed cost) base of the company. When product profitability is analysed, it is expected to apportion an element of overhead to its cost, which should then be charged out via the sales price. Overheads are the support for the infrastructure upon which the operations of the business can run, so it makes sense that a proportion of total overheads should be allocated to each unit of production.

The method of overhead apportionment will largely depend on the company, though the concept is the same regardless of the driver. The driver is the cost element upon which the overhead apportionment will be based. The most common method is to divide the total overhead value by total sales and apportion overheads to each type of product based on volume sales. This is displayed in the example shown in Table 6.6.

In the following example, a company has three products for the month of January totalling £5,020. The calculated volume of products to be produced was based on last year's sales trends. The company has overheads of £1,000, which were apportioned to each product based on percentage of total sales.

Table 6.6   Product profitability statement

Product profitability statement for the period January 2007				
	Product 1	**Product 2**	**Product 3**	**Total Products**
Unit sales		100	76	250	
Sales £ per unit		10	20	10	
Income		1,000	1,520	2,500	5,020
Direct costs		(500)	(608)	(1,500)	(2,608)
Gross profit		500	912	1,000	2,412
Overheads	1000	200	302	498	1,000
OAR	% of total sales				
Net profit		300	610	502	1,412
Ranking (1 highest profitability)		3	1	2	

The output from Table 6.6 tells management that product 2 is actually the most profitable and therefore resources should be put into that product until demand is satisfied. The resources of the company should then be used to manufacture product 3 and lastly product 1. This analysis depends on customer demand and operational bottlenecks, both of which should be investigated before a full business decision can be made on this management information.

Key performance indicators (KPI)

The MAP should provide in numerical, written and graphical format the key performance indicators (KPI) of a company. These are factors which drive areas of the company such as sales, profitability and efficiency. Again, the focus should be on reporting those KPI that are specific to a company.

Case study

When the MAP for Bed Co was set up, the directors were asked for their top six information needs. So, when the KPI page was created, it included the data that they felt was needed to monitor their business effectively:

- profitability of each unit produced;
- sales by product, both core (beds) and accessory products;
- the time it took to deliver on an order once placed by the customer;
- efficiency of their asset base;
- hours of management time spent on core activities;
- overall company profitability.

Each of these requirements was easily analysed and was instantly added to the MAP, to provide a clear picture of how their business was performing. While each business will require different information, there are basic business analysis ratios and formula that are applicable to the majority of small businesses.

The following ratios provide the SME owner/manager with the tools to answer questions, such as those posed by the Bed Co directors. Before selecting the ratios, write down 10 questions that the company directors and management want answered about the business. These 10 questions and answers should be included in the MAP along with the P&L, balance sheet and cashflow statement.

Here are some possible questions (and answers) that you may have about your business, together with ratios or formula that will provide an answer to the question.

Q: How useful are the assets that are on the balance sheet?
Asset turnover per period = sales / total assets

Q: How profitable are the sales of the company?
Return on sales = net income / sales

Q: How well is a specific investment performing?
Return on capital employed = (profit / capital employed) * 100%

Q: How efficient is our labour force?
Labour costs / total costs of production

Q: What kind of return are we getting from our annual marketing spend?
Marketing and promotional costs / sales

Think about the type of analysis you want to carry out on your business and use a fixed ratio or financial equation to provide the information you need. We covered performance measuring tools in more detail in Chapter 5 on decision making.

Chart of accounts

Set up the chart of accounts (in your nominal ledger) to reflect the accounting categories in the P&L and balance sheet. This will save time when performing the statutory reporting and will ensure that the business is correctly capturing and accounting for each transaction made by the company.

The chart of accounts should be set up to reflect the nature of the business. Reporting requirements, such as departmental analysis, should also be considered at this stage as it may impact on how the nominal ledger coding is structured.

Conclusion

SMEs should produce a bespoke MAP for their business. The accurate use of ratios and other management accounting tools aids management to review financial performance, trends and variances by using historic data to plan for future events. The figures in the MAP should also be compared with competitor information, where possible, to identify strengths and weaknesses and to ensure the company is acting competitively.

An effective company MAP will provide all users with the information they need while remaining clear and concise. Once created, continue to review the needs of the stakeholders who actively use the MAP to make business decisions.

Key points to remember

- A management accounting pack, or MAP, should be used by every company to report on past performance and make future decisions about the business.
- Key uses and users of the MAP.
- When setting up a MAP for your company, consider the needs of the parties who will use the report.
- Contents of a MAP:
  - profit and loss statement (P&L);
  - balance sheet;
  - capital and reserves;
  - cashflow statement;
  - product profitability statement;
  - key performance indictors (KPI);
  - other relevant information bespoke to your business.
- Use quantitative analysis reported in the MAP to answer key questions relevant to the business, such as:
  - How useful are the assets on the balance sheet?
  - How profitable are the sales of the company?
  - How well is a specific investment performing?
  - How efficient is our labour force?
  - What kind of return are we getting from our annual marketing spend?

7

Organisational management

Organisational management is an area in a small business that is often not given the attention it deserves. There is such a focus on delivery of products that sometimes one of the key resources involved in its delivery, labour (people), can be overlooked. SMEs should consider organisational management theories and techniques as important to their overall performance as do large companies with hundreds of employees.

Another term for organisational management is human resource management. Employees are human and therefore have basic needs that must be satisfied. Meanwhile, employees are a valuable resource of the company, and therefore should be utilised to maximise profits. These two concepts do not always go hand in hand and there is often a balance to be found between employee satisfaction and maximised efficiency. Once a company has found an approach to organisational management that can provide this balance, the positive impact on financial performance should be easily quantifiable.

As with many of the subjects we cover in this book, the scope of organisational management is vast and cannot be covered in detail in the space available – and, in the context of an SME, there is no need. The owner/manager needs to be aware of the following basic concepts:

- how to use labour in a cost-effective way;
- organisational structure;
- importance of the finance function;
- organisational behaviour – problem solving;

- factors that affect job satisfaction and its impact on the efficiency of the company;
- importance of organisational management policies.

Once these factors are appreciated by the manager, the approach to better organisational management should be generated internally to improve staff behaviour and performance with the ultimate objective of maximising profits.

Relevance of management accounting to organisational management

Labour is expensive and it will often be the single largest expense in a company. There are management accounting methods that can apply to the SME to ensure that the labour resource is operating efficiently.

Small businesses generally can't afford a dedicated human resources manager, therefore the role tends to fall to the finance manager or accountant. Organisational management is not just a matter of handing out job descriptions. This chapter aims to provide an insight into practical organisational management relevant to a small business environment.

Labour productivity analysis

In most SMEs, there are two types of labour – fixed and variable. When carrying out labour productivity analysis, management should first create a labour resource plan. This would normally cover only the variable labour: the employees or contractors whose labour can be directly attributed to the production and/or continuing service of the goods which are sold by the company. Variable labour could include those who work in sales and in operations such as manufacturing and customer care.

Labour capacity should be driven by unit production in that increased demand for the product drives increased unit production and therefore an increased labour resource is required. Unit production is a more efficient driver of sales and, therefore, profits. The total cost of labour should be broken down based on its requirements per unit produced.

For example, 100 hours are spent on two different products and costs run at £5 per hour. Product A requires 50 hours to make 200 units (4 units per hour), whereas Product B requires 50 hours to make 250 units (5 units per hour). Product A, therefore, has a unit labour cost of £1.25 (£5/4 units per hour) and Product B has a unit labour cost of £1 (£5/5 units per hour). This labour price per unit should be factored into the costing of each unit, and should therefore be included in the overall sales price of a unit.

Once the labour resource plan has been created and agreed, employees can then be hired or reallocated depending on the company's requirements and their relevant skill sets. Labour productivity can be measured in many ways; however, the simplest and most proven method is the ratio of labour costs as a percentage of total production costs: Labour costs / Production costs.*

Case study

M Ltd, an advertising agency, found that they were using different levels and grades of labour for different jobs. When analysis was carried out on the overall job profitability, the labour cost was never factored in, thus giving incomplete information and an overstated view of client and project profitability. Management had to set up a labour productivity analysis from scratch before it could be included as a component in their overall client and project profitability figures – which are the drivers for overall company performance.

The first step was to improve data capture by ensuring that all labour resources – both internal and external – started filling out timesheets. This was not initially accepted by the staff as they felt that management were acting in an invasive manner. The knock-on effect of their continued reluctance to account for their time was explained as follows – no labour data in profitability leads to over-stated client profitability, which leads to over-stated company profits, which leads to distorted working capital data, which can

---

* NB: To obtain a production costs figure, define a project or production area that you wish to use as the basis of the labour productivity analysis. It is important to be able to ring-fence and quantify the area for analysis clearly.

lead to bad business decisions leading to worsening company per-formance, which can lead to job losses. Once they understood the importance of the data, they grudgingly provided the timekeeping data required for the labour analysis.

It is important to encourage employees to understand why they must start accounting for their time. It is not unusual to encounter a certain amount of reluctance from staff. Communication of the overall reason behind the change in process should help to overcome these initial attitudes.

The data required from timesheets is generally:

- client (or customer);
- specific project (or product) name;
- summary details of task performed;
- hours (or days) spent per task.

Once M Ltd's staff completed the timesheets, the time data was then quantified by multiplying the hours worked by the hourly rate paid to the labour resource by the company. Management now had the total labour cost that would be allocated to the clients or projects. Note that this is not the same as the total labour cost for the business. It is understood that people need downtime for eating, relaxing and general administrative tasks. Always take data from specific client or project timekeeping tools rather than the company's profit and loss statement.

Allocate the time recorded by each employee to a client or project – this figure becomes the labour cost. To complete the analysis, we now needed the total costs per client or project. These should be allocated to the client or project when entered into the accounting system. Once all direct costs for each client and project had been collected, the labour productivity ratio was calculated.

The labour productivity ratio on its own doesn't have much relevance. Like any ratio, its importance and relevance as a management tool is realised when it is compared with the same project from period to period or in the same period against different projects. Decisions of efficiency and modification to a company's labour resource should be based on this labour productivity analysis.

Organisational structure

When deciding upon the organisational structure of the company, it is important to consider the objectives and how best to manage the available resources, in this case labour, to best achieve those objectives.

A basic organisation model can be applied to any SME, to aid information systems and development of the organisational structure and culture of a company. The model shown in Figure 7.1 is a good reminder of how critical individual employees are to the overall company objective. It's worth noting how all of the company functions are linked with the thoughts, feelings and behaviour of the employees, who lie at the core of the company's operations. There is also a direct link from external factors to the employees which can impact on the company.

Flat organisational structure

While there are many types of organisational structure, most SMEs are likely to adopt a flat structure, which, for the purposes of a small company, is likely to have three tiers.

There is one most senior manager, usually titled managing director (MD), who sits at tier one of the structure. The MD's priority is overall strategy of the company and to deliver shareholder objectives. Tier two houses the managers of the main areas of the company who report directly to the MD – these are usually the operations director (OD), the information director (ID) and the finance director (FD). Each of these roles will have one or a number of individuals reporting to them on operational issues – these people sit in tier three. Occasionally, a small business will have more tiers under tier three, though this will depend on the company and often creates unnecessary bureaucracy.

Bear in mind that the type of operational director mentioned here is in name only – they are not necessarily a statutory director of the company by holding a title appointed to them by the company. An operational director need not be a statutory director, and similarly a statutory director need not hold a senior management post within the company.

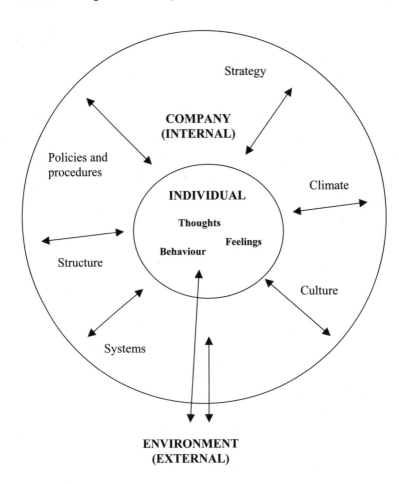

Figure 7.1 Basic organisational model

The terms (MD, FD etc) used here are British terminology. In recent years, we have seen American organisational terminology creep into British business jargon, for example chief executive officer (CEO) in the place of MD. Sometimes they are used within the same company, for example a CFO reporting to an MD. Choose one type of terminology and apply it throughout the organisation.

This flat organisation structure, which is generally best practice for a small business environment, is represented in Figure 7.2.

We will now look at the finance function in some detail, the importance of which is often misunderstood or underestimated by general managers.

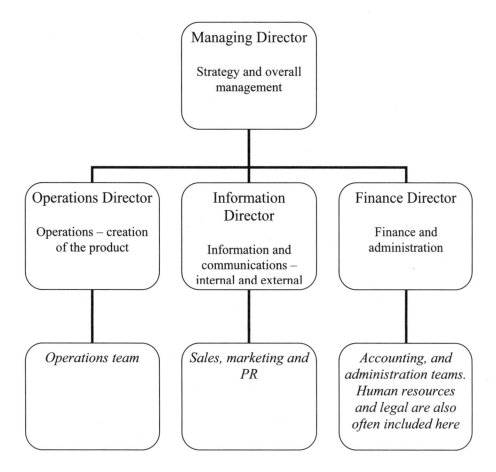

Figure 7.2   Organisational structure of a small business

Importance of the finance function

Amazingly, many businesses try to operate without dedicated financial support. Some are successful despite this; however, many failed businesses can directly attribute their failure to insufficient financial support.

There is more to running a successful business than adding up some till receipts at the end of the day and paying bills when they come in the post. There is an element of control, information and expertise that good financial support brings to a business. Many of the small business owners I have started supporting didn't have an accountant – which was evident from the lack of controls and management in the company. The main reason for this seemed to be the perception of cost. It is true that an internal accounting resource isn't cheap and if you are trying to set up a business on a shoestring, a qualified accountant on the books isn't going to make financial sense.

However, there is a strong cost–benefit analysis argument for employing a dedicated resource who focuses on the financial strength of your business and helps management plan throughout the different life cycles of the company. If management have financial training or experience, then this is perhaps not necessary at the early stages; however, generally the benefits of an accounting resource cannot be underestimated.

Case study

Telecoms Co was set up by a long-serving member of the telecoms environment in the UK and abroad – an industry big-hitter. When he started out on his own, he didn't anticipate the need for financial support. It was not long until I had a phone call from the slightly overwhelmed director, panicked by the paperwork needed in relation to the Inland Revenue, VAT compliance and the difficulty of working capital management. He was able to admit that he could not fill every task in a corporate environment and asked me to join him on a part-time basis to set up some processes and make sure that everything was running as effectively as possible.

First, he found that the company was actually better off financially as the cost of the financial support to the business was offset by the increase of sales achieved by using increased working capital generated through use of credit terms and the application of other management accounting techniques. A further benefit of increased working capital reserves was that he could buy more units more profitably, maximising economies of scale, and take the margin as profit. The director also found that he had more time to think about the business because he wasn't worrying whether or not the taxman's requirements were being satisfied and he now knew that his business was being run efficiently from a financial perspective.

Just how much support do you need?

The amount of financial support required is contingent upon the background of management and the size and the complexity of the business. Most start-ups and SMEs require a part-time bookkeeper and an experienced, more senior accountant once a month, with an aim to manage financial performance indicators. You will soon work out what works for you and your company.

Financial support requirements depend on the size and complexity of your business. Finance staff range in education, qualification, experience and therefore cost. Figure 7.3 depicts a typical finance department structure.

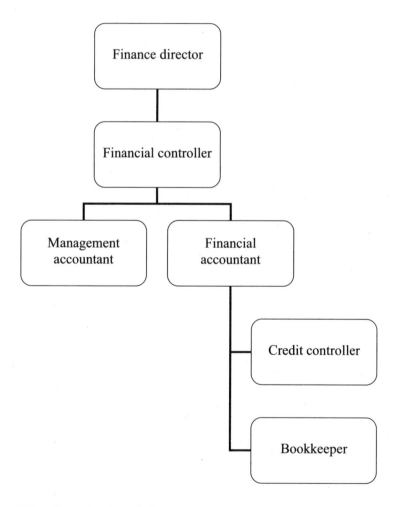

Figure 7.3   Organisational chart – finance department

Finance director

The finance director focuses on strategic decisions and financial planning based on the information provided by the financial controller. Tax and corporate finance initiatives should originate with the finance director. Often the finance department also has the functions of administration and human resources under their umbrella, so the finance director should also manage these functions accordingly.

Financial controller

The financial controller will oversee the members of the team to ensure that processes and controls are being adhered to and that the data and information provided are timely, accurate and presented in the required format. The financial controller will often report to the finance director on the operations and financial detail of the business.

Management accountant

The management accountant will prepare the management accounting pack (MAP) from the financial reports prepared by the financial accountant. This will include statistical data and variance analysis which will be the information upon which the senior finance and management team can make business decisions.

Financial accountant

The financial accountant uses the information collated during the month by the credit controller and bookkeeper as a basis to prepare the financial accounts, ie profit and loss statement, balance sheet, cashflow statements and any other financial statements necessary to the business. Month-end adjustments in the accounts such as accruals, prepayments and other journal entries will be made by the financial accountant, sometimes in discussion with the management accountant to ensure that all relevant data has been captured.

Bookkeeper

A bookkeeper checks and logs all sales and purchase invoices and other relevant accounting entries to present a trial balance ready for month-end adjustments and analysis. They should also reconcile the bank accounts and ensure all transactions are correct and accounted for.

Credit controller

The credit control function controls money due to the business from customers. Their method and relationship with your customers can be critical when relying on cash inflows and prompt payment on sales invoices.

In small companies many, if not all, of the above functions can be merged in one role. Often the ideal financial person to have on board with a start-up or SME is an accountant who can make strategic decisions, but also doesn't mind posting invoices and doing the bank reconciliation. Again, you will soon realise the needs of your business, but it's important to realise the benefits that come with having solid financial support.

Employees will generally be looking to their employer to advance their own careers and maximise their rewards by way of salary, experience and other benefits. They will weigh up the benefit of working for you against working for an alternative employer and will generally choose the most self-serving option. There are exceptions, of course, but generally this is how employees approach their careers. Through the promotion of goal congruence, management can get the best out of their employees while motivating their labour resource to operate in the method most effective for the business. Set common goals and monitor them to ensure that the employee is working to best serve the company's objectives.

Organisational behaviour – problem solving

People are unpredictable, so your business may encounter a situation with an employee that is not ideal for the smooth operation of the business. Identify and solve the problem immediately. Examples of problematic organisational behaviour include inefficiency, personality clashes within a team, mistakes from ineptitude or poor training and even employee theft.

Problem solving within organisational management can be approached using three very simple steps – define the problem, analyse the detail and extent of the problem and undertake action planning to solve the problem.

Step 1: Define the problem

Start by finding the source of the problem. Perhaps you have been made aware of the problem through direct contact or you discovered it through business analysis. If the problem is significant enough that senior management have an awareness of the issues, it certainly must be remedied. A problem of organisational behaviour, in this context, is a condition that is adversely impacting on the performance of the business and will continue to do so. The source of the problem must be targeted, otherwise the situation will continue, with detrimental effects to the company, its performance and perhaps external perception.

Try to apply some level of priority to the problem – is it urgent and requiring immediate action or can it wait to be thoroughly investigated prior to the application of a solution? Find the most important problems within the situation and aim to solve these first. Make sure that you can recognise the source from the symptoms – symptoms stem from the source and will continue unless the source problem is completely resolved.

Step 2: Analyse the problem

Once the source of the problem has been identified, it should be linked with a gap in the process that allowed the source to occur in the first place. Without establishing the causal link, the source could re-establish itself.

Step 3: Solve the problem

Once the source of the problem has been found and removed, thus ensuring that it will not return once resolved, management should take active steps to solve the problem. The key for management is to be proactive, as it is rare that problems sort themselves out. Ignoring the actual situation that has been created by organisational behaviour will not solve the problem.

Action planning should be formally set out by a designated manager who will set goals for the task and define his or her approach. A timeframe should be set for this problem to be solved, and all endeavours, where they do not detract from the normal operations of the business, should be applied to the task.

The process should be a learning experience for those involved to help promote the situation not recurring. If appropriate, the solution process should be transparent to the company to ensure that correct information about the problem and its solution is communicated around the company. Prevention of speculation on such issues is better than a cure for misinformation.

Case study

Music Co had an employee who had been at the company for many years. When new management came in to take control of the company it was decided to retain this employee as she had a good knowledge of the history of the company, which they thought would be useful. It was soon obvious that the employee was not trained in new systems and processes and was very slow. She was also resistant to any changes that were introduced and kept performing tasks as she had been doing for 23 years, despite the fact that the company was moving on around her. The situation came to the attention of the directors through the staff working closely with this employee, as she created a bottleneck in the output of their department.

The directors agreed that steps needed to be taken as her performance was adversely impacting the performance and profitability of the company. They followed the three-step plan of problem solving by first defining the problem. They discreetly questioned staff working with her and her manager. It was clear that she was in her job purely because nobody had the heart to let her go.

Analysing the problem included interviewing the employee and suggesting retraining and support to bring her up to speed. She refused and therefore the third step, solving the problem, was to give her notice as she was not performing her duties as per her contract.

This was a difficult situation for management; however, by following the three steps of problem solving, they knew that all factors had been taken into consideration and that they had made the best decision for the company.

Factors that impact on job satisfaction

A very common organisational problem is that of employee motivation and job satisfaction, and the resulting employee behaviour and retention. The next section of this chapter will look in more detail at these issues and will highlight specific factors of which a small business manager should be aware.

While management accounting provides analysis tools with which to plan and measure labour resources, an effective manager should also consider the impact of the job satisfaction of employees and the financial impact of employee behaviour on profitability. There's no need to become a psychologist, but I have found that it does help for managers to have an awareness of what motivates their staff.

Goal congruence

Earlier in the chapter we referred to goal congruence. This is a concept whereby both parties in a situation have the same objectives and will therefore act with the interest of achieving that objective. In this case, the two parties are the employees and the employer. Align the employees' objectives with that of the company and the management of staff to perform their duties efficiently will become much less problematic.

A common example of this is to align the remuneration of the sales team with the profitability of the company. If the company performs in line with budget, the sales team is rewarded. When possible, ensure that the driver of goal congruence is profits, not sales turnover, as this could create behaviour that could be detrimental to the financial performance of the company. Targets should be set for the benefit of shareholders' equity, so look at what is best for the company overall, not just in the short term.

Salespeople are often difficult to manage and motivate as they can be working remotely and therefore may not benefit from the corporate culture of the company. The influence of goal congruence over their behaviour will become a key motivator which will act as a management tool over their activities.

What is job satisfaction?

The definition of job satisfaction largely depends on the understanding of individual employee attitudes and motivations. It is essential for a manager to understand what drives an individual to pursue success and continue to achieve in their chosen career.

Job satisfaction can be defined as a positive emotional state. This is affected by the gap between intended and actual performance, being the degree to which one's performance meets with one's own set of professional and ethical values, and many other tangible and intangible behavioural characteristics.

While the importance of factors such as organisational commitment and goal congruence have been found to impact directly on job satisfaction, it has also been shown through research that such factors may not override the basic need for expected individual remuneration levels and the need for basic recognition. In other words, pay and praise tend to be the biggest motivators for employees.

Importance of organisational citizenship

Employees develop a social identity that ties them into both their chosen profession and their organisation. Through this social identity, employees align themselves with the culture of an organisation, which promotes the concept of organisational citizenship. In identifying with a company, employees are relying on their employer to satisfy basic needs such as suitable working conditions and tasks, pay equity and training. In this case, employees feel that they are part of the common destiny of the company for success or failure.

Lower levels of organisational commitment can lead to decreased levels of job satisfaction. There is a need for the company to invest in their employees to ensure that this feeling of organisational commitment is retained. Belief in social and corporate obligations is of high importance to employees and indeed has been proven to outweigh other motivators, with the possible exception of financial reward.

Inter-role conflict

Employees experience inter-role conflict when incompatibility arises in the role they must fill for their company and the ethical values and constraints of either their own professional bodies or their own personal moral code.

A recent survey in the UK found that a high percentage of employees find job satisfaction through role congruence (an absence of inter-role conflict) and where this is jeopardised, lower levels of job satisfaction exist. Inter-role conflict is associated with low job satisfaction and a high propensity to leave a company, which can lead to decreased financial performance.

Management should be more supportive of an employee's role autonomy and minimise demands of corporate culture with a view to increasing job satisfaction. Inter-role conflict can lead to many negative consequences for the employee and the overall culture of the company, unless managed effectively.

Importance of organisational management policies

The application of organisational management can be a decisive factor in the success of the company, as it promotes a culture of developing and retaining quality employees. While employees can be self-motivating and self-regulating, there is evidence to suggest that a successful organisational management policy can promote increased job satisfaction, which in turn reduces the likelihood of intent to leave, which is costly for a small business.

It has been established that inter-role conflict and lower levels of commitment to an employer lead to lower levels of job satisfaction. It is, therefore, recommended that management ensure that the employee feels supported by the business. This is certainly the case with SMEs, as employees may perceive that training and career support would be better in a larger company. This investment in staff can be expensive for a small business; however, it is important to ensure that your staff feel as though their needs are being met. Remember, it is much more expensive to recruit and retrain than to retain a well-performing employee.

Turnover of employees is a major cost and burden to any organisation. Lower levels of organisational commitment and job satisfaction can lead directly to an intent to leave the organisation. An inexpensive method to apply to this dilemma is for a company to have better defined employee roles, which should help to clarify employee and corporate objectives.

Management should focus on providing the desired culture and management influence to motivate employees to retain a high level of job satisfaction. Companies generally look to shape desirable employee attitudes through an organisational culture.

Company culture

A company with a positive corporate culture will enjoy many benefits. Employees working for companies with a positive culture will generally have higher morale and will show increased levels of teamwork, communication, learning and performance. Indeed, many companies who have achieved a positive working environment use their culture to gain a competitive advantage in their industry. Chapter 4 provides more detail on competitive advantage through effective use of resources. In contrast, a poor or neglected emphasis on company culture can lead to job dissatisfaction and ultimately decreased financial performance.

One of the main influences on company culture is style of management. All SMEs wishing to improve employee relations should first review the effectiveness and attitudes of their managers at all levels. Participation in decision making and empowerment is strongly positively correlated with work-related outcomes. This would suggest that it is an employee's relationship with their boss and the way that they are managed that provides the best indication of personal job satisfaction, role congruence and customer satisfaction.

Importance of management styles

Of all the factors that a firm can control to retain staff longer, often one of the easiest areas to improve is the approach taken by management towards its employees. A corporate culture that emphasises teamwork and cohesion rather than rigid procedures and work quotas is more likely to retain its employees (and its training investment) longer. This results in minimising the upheaval that follows rapid staff turnover.

Management styles differ and some may be appropriate where others are likely to fail. SMEs are more likely to have a flat corporate structure with a relatively autocratic management style, where power is held by a single person. If a small business has started life with one manager and four employees, it can be hard for that one manager to delegate power. It is often the case that after a period of growth, the manager attempts to maintain his or her control over operations and decision-making situations which should be distributed among the expanding workforce. There will be times when a change in management style will benefit the company.

Management styles

Four of the most common management styles to be found in an SME are autonomous, permissive, coercive and management by objectives.

Autonomous management

- Employees are given little room for initiative.
- One manager controls detailed operations.
- Employee resentment is often found, owing to lack of opportunity to be creative.
- This is the style used by most entrepreneurial start-ups, though it should evolve as the company grows. Quite often the autonomous manager finds delegation difficult and continues to employ an autonomous management style long after it is appropriate to do so.

Permissive management

- The opposite of autonomous in that employees have a high degree of autonomy.
- Employees are allowed to take part in the management of operations and input at a strategic level.
- The team makes decisions unilaterally.
- This is quite often the management style that small companies adopt during their mature stage of development.
- Management structure can become too loose with loss of accountability, so if a permissive style of management is adopted, ensure that there remains a clear line of authority.

Coercive management

- This form of management style is used in fiercely competitive environments, such as sales, where employees are target driven.
- Motivation is by threat of punishment by formal reprimands or removal of benefits.
- Managers exert power through their unique competence or specific knowledge, but often through an employee's fear of failure or punishment.

■ There are very few small company situations where a coercive management style can be successful. When it is applied in the appropriate environment, however, it can be the only approach that will be effective owing to the nature of the employees and their working environment. Unless the situation obviously requires an approach of this nature, its application would be a risky proposition.

Management by objectives

■ This is a very popular method used by small businesses.
■ It promotes goal congruence – if the company performs well, so does the employee.
■ Management should set key performance targets to motivate the employee.
■ It provides a direct link from strategic objectives to the operations of individual employees.
■ It promotes communication and awareness of the overall objectives and performance of the company, also leading to enhanced motivation.

Case study

Recruit Co was started by one director using his own capital and, in the first year, he had only one assistant to help with the operation and growth of the business. His business did very well. At the end of the fourth year, he had grown the company to 47 staff over three offices. Yet he still tried to do everything himself and wanted to sign off on every decision – regardless of its actual impact on the business. One example I saw was when this director wanted to sign off on a change in stationery supplier. At this point, I asked him what he wanted from the business; his response was further growth but he needed to have enough time to devote to strategy. It was time for him to let go. We reviewed types of management styles and looked at those staff around him – many of whom were becoming frustrated at the lack of initiative the company allowed them.

The director agreed to formally set a management tier of three trusted and proven employees underneath him to whom he could delegate. It took a little time for him to feel that he could let go, but he did and the company thrived as a result, because he now had the time to spend on the strategic direction and growth of the company.

Sometimes we can't see what is obvious to others as there is no time to stop and take stock of the situation. Make time, and remember to ask those around you what they think.

Conclusion

When considering the organisation management of the company, don't leave the management of employees to chance or think that it will take care of itself. In the absence of management, employees will inevitably take care of themselves, but that may not be in the best interest of the company's objectives and overall strategic focus. Think about what employees need and want from the company and apply this information when forming a labour resource strategy and operational plan. A well-managed and motivated workforce will undoubtedly benefit the SME financially, but should also create a company that is a fun and dynamic place to work.

Key points to remember

- Organisation management deserves management attention and time as employees (labour) are often one of the largest costs to a small business.
- Employees are a valuable resource and should be used effectively to maximise profits. Organisational management skills are important to ensure that this resource is managed well.
- Labour productivity analysis is a useful tool for the small business:
  - Identify fixed and variable labour.
  - Ensure time spent on specific tasks is captured using timesheets.
  - Calculate hourly or daily rates per employee to provide a resource cost.
  - Multiply unit cost by time spent to obtain labour productivity detail.

- Organisational structure: a flat structure is generally the best practice for a small company.
- Importance of the finance function.
- Problem solving – organisation behaviour issues:
  - Step 1: Define the problem.
  - Step 2: Analyse the problem.
  - Step 3: Solve the problem.
- Factors that impact on job satisfaction include:
  - goal congruence;
  - motivation;
  - remuneration;
  - organisational citizenship;
  - absence of inter-role conflict.
- Management styles include:
  - autonomous;
  - permissive;
  - coercive;
  - management by objectives.

8

Project management

Most small businesses at some point in their lives will enter into a project outside the scope of their day-to-day activities. Such projects could include testing of a new product, expansion into new premises or an employee satisfaction audit. There are many examples of projects that a company will decide to action. While, for the purposes of this chapter, a project will be considered an undertaking outside the normal operations of a company, they still require funding from the company' s working capital, so it is important to ensure that the project will use resources effectively.

The first step when embarking on a project is to ensure that it will have some economic benefit to the company – either now or in the future. The techniques for this analysis, such as decision trees, are covered in Chapter 5. Remember that a project need not deliver direct financial rewards. The improvement of staff morale, for example, could be the outcome of a project deemed worthy by management, though its impact on profitability will be indirect and often unquantifiable.

The relevance of management accounting to project management

Project management requires attention to detail and a focused mind, not to mention access to financial and operational information on the company and its relevant stakeholders. A small company will often rely on management accounting techniques to provide this data required for effective project management.

When should an initiative be treated as a project?

A lack of detail often leads to misunderstanding, which can result in the loss of company resources. If an initiative looks as if it might be sufficiently detailed to require a formal plan, then it should be treated as a project.

Also, a project format is much more effective when there are multiple parties involved in the process, as it aids communication. Project management is designed to capture and report information as well as monitor the time and money spent on its activities. A formal structure can enhance the output and communication of a project over that of an *ad hoc* approach.

Project management constraints

Traditionally, there are three constraints which will, in varying degrees, impact on the progress and outcome of the project. These limitations are time, cost and scope. These three constraints are often referred to as the 'project management triangle' as they are linked and dependent on each other to deliver the overall project (Figure 8.1). An action on one side of the triangle

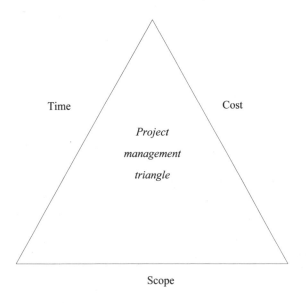

Figure 8.1   Project management triangle

will impact on another, so all three elements must be considered in equal measure for each project decision taken.

Time

Project time should be calculated and reported in terms of time units, normally hours or days, depending on the required detail of financial output. For large-scale projects, days are sufficient, though smaller projects should be reported in terms of hours. A time unit should report time employed or billed to a project.

When accounting for internal labour, attach a value to each time unit based on the cost of that employee to the business. Total gross salary, tax, national insurance and any other benefits paid to the employee and divide this by the number of time units available. This provides a time unit cost. Chapter 7 has further information on labour productivity analysis and the importance of timesheets to capture data. The employee should provide a timesheet of all time spent on the project. External consultants should provide an invoice to the company detailing time spent by task and any other category required, such as by client or department.

Project management tasks should be broken down into time blocks, ie how much time it will take to complete each main section of the project. Once this analysis has been carried out, each section should be broken down into tasks and time requirements allocated to each task. If there is a further breakdown required within each task, then a further sub-allocation of time should be made.

Cost

When costing a project prior to its commencement, it is important to capture all relevant costs. Relevant costs are defined in Chapter 5. These will normally include labour, materials, equipment and machinery. There may be a number of other factors dependent of the type of project.

Once cost estimates have been established, factor in the required profit (if applicable). If the project has a profit motive, this, along with the costs, should be monitored throughout the life of the project and actions taken when forward analysis indicates that actual profits may fall short of the original objective. Forward analysis is simply using current or historical data to make assumptions about future performance.

Scope

The scope of the project is its overall objective and the elements required to achieve the objective. A specific description should be sufficiently detailed for all of the individuals included in the project management team to understand the objectives and how the project will achieve its aim. Details such as the level of quality, number of units, and use of output and resource requirements should also be included.

The scope should monitor the costs and time, just as the time constraints should ensure that the costs and scope are maintained – hence the concept of the project management triangle.

Project management models

There are many models used by companies to manage their projects, though not all are relevant to an SME as they are far too detailed and onerous for the relatively limited resources of a smaller project team. The following models can be used and adapted by a project manager within an SME to provide the desired results effectively. While not all of these models will be well suited to every project, it is certainly beneficial to have a working knowledge of each of the following management accounting techniques used by project managers. This will enable the project manager to select the best-suited method for each specific project in order to maximise the quality of the output and efficient use of resources.

Gantt chart

By far the most popular and easy-to-use project management tool, the Gantt chart is used by businesses to track the progression of each stage of a project. Even while writing this book, I have created a Gantt chart to monitor the chapters written and their appropriate stage of review. It is a flexible tool which can be used for the smallest project lasting a week to a large-scale project running over a year.

The Gantt chart is a scheduling tool presented in a horizontal bar graph format, with the horizontal axis being time (Figure 8.2). The time units on the chart will depend on the length of the project; for example, use weekly units for a three-month project or monthly for a two-year project. The vertical axis should indicate the tasks within the project – the detailed level of which

TASK DETAIL	TEAM MANAGER	TEAM MEMBERS	24-Dec	31-Dec	07-Jan	14-Jan	21-Jan	28-Jan	04-Feb	11-Feb	18-Feb	25-Feb	04-Mar	11-Mar	18-Mar	25-Mar
Task 1			1											3		
Task 2				1						2				3		
Task 3				1						2				3		
Task 4				1							2			3		
Task 5					1						2	2			3	
Task 6					1							2			3	
Task 7						1							2			3
Task 8													2			3
Task 9							1						2			3

MILESTONE KEY

1	*Phase 1 of the project*
2	*Phase 2 of the project*
3	*Phase 3 of the project*

Figure 8.2 Gantt chart – example

will be project dependent. A horizontal bar across the relevant time units will indicate when a specific activity should occur and conclude.

An additional feature to use on the Gantt chart is milestones. Management accounting reports will often require information on what percentage of a project has been completed. The use of milestones will enable this calculation to be made easily.

The Gantt chart is useful in an SME as it is easy to produce and update. It also provides the status of a project at a glance and is therefore a useful graphical tool to use in a pack of information, such as the MAP as covered in Chapter 6, where significant information might be lost in the detail. It does, however, have its limits owing to its relatively unsophisticated format.

Process analysis

A project is made up of many processes which, when consolidated produce the desired objectives from the original plan. Process analysis is a method of managing a series of inputs into a process to ensure that the output is of the quality and specification required by the initiator of the project.

Inputs into the process would normally include labour, materials and capital items. Examples of output could include the specified end product, from an idea or concept to a finished product. The most common use for process analysis within an SME environment is for work in progress (WIP) management whereby raw materials (input) are worked to become the finished, saleable product (output). Every company with an element of manufacturing should apply process analysis to the WIP cycle.

The application of a framework to manage and monitor a process can have a significant positive impact on the company's financial performance and can reduce its risk and exposure to competition.

The following tasks should be carried out when using process analysis for project management:

- Identify the inputs required for the process.
- Allocate a time during the process where these inputs will be required.
- Identify where the outputs of the process will be realised.
- Create a process analysis diagram to map the inputs and output on a time line; this should display the activities within the process and their level of co-dependency.

- Calculate the capacity in each process to ensure that it is able to meet its demands.
- Bottlenecks, the areas of lowest capacity which restrict process flow, should identify themselves as a result of this capacity analysis. We will look at bottlenecks in more detail later in this chapter.
- The overall process analysis is designed to enable well-informed management decisions and process improvements.

The symbols used in a process flow diagram are shown in Figure 8.3.

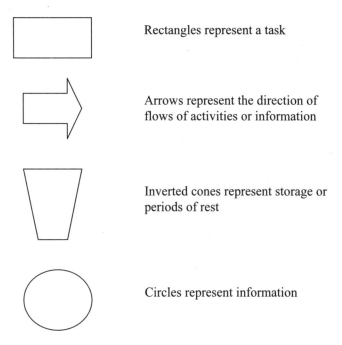

Rectangles represent a task

Arrows represent the direction of flows of activities or information

Inverted cones represent storage or periods of rest

Circles represent information

Figure 8.3   Process flow symbols

Process flow diagram

The above procedure requires a process analysis diagram to be created to monitor the input and output capacity and movement. The diagrammatical analysis is very easy to create and to manage.

The actual diagram is a time line made up of graphical elements to reflect each process within the overall project. The complexity of the process flow diagram will depend on the amount, type and level of interactivity between each process.

Process flow diagram – practical example

Bed Co is a small business that uses process analysis to project manage the creation of their products – bespoke beds. A customer will place an order for a bed and Bed Co will then buy in the raw materials required for its production. The production has three processes that occur sequentially – preparing the raw materials for assembly, the actual assembly and finishing the bed with decoration required by the customer. There is a fourth process that requires the accessories for the bed to be made, which occurs just before the actual assembly of the bed. This process then provides its own output: the finished accessories. The output of the first production sequence is the finished bed.

While each individual process in itself involves more detail than the process analysis provides, the directors find it useful to have an overall picture of the process. Let's look at how this process would be displayed (Figure 8.4).

Bed Co manufacturing process:

1.	Customer order placed
2.	Buy raw materials
3.	Production – prepare raw materials for assembly
4.	Production – assembly
5.	Production – finishing
6.	Order accessories
7.	Deliver accessories
8.	Deliver finished product

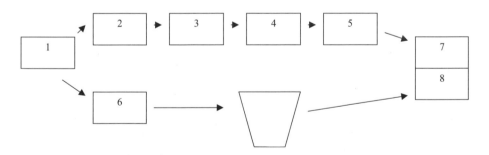

Note that the accessories must be stored while the production process is taking place as Bed Co order the accessories upon customer order to ensure they can be delivered with the finished product.

Figure 8.4   Process flow diagram (Bed Co)

Process analysis is best used for processes that flow sequentially and that are clearly defined. When constructing a process flow diagram, ensure that each process has been analysed to ensure that input requirements and capacity issues have been correctly calculated. The accuracy of the entire process could be called into question if one process has been miscalculated, as there is a high level of interdependence between each process.

Bottlenecks

Where a process in the chain does not have capacity to deal with the level of inputs, it should be classed a bottleneck, which is the slowest or least-capacity process in the cycle. Once the bottleneck has been identified, the process should then be modified to enable the limited capacity process to meet the level of input or outputs. The effect of the bottleneck should be quantified to establish any opportunity cost of not improving the process to negate the capacity problem. A management decision should then be based on the cost/benefit of correcting the bottleneck process.

Process constraint remedies

If the cost–benefit analysis of a bottleneck process indicates that the increase in outputs would sufficiently cover the cost of unblocking the capacity constraint, there are process improvements available as remedy, including:

- Spread out the inputs over a greater time period, provided it does not adversely impact on the overall output.
- Improve the efficiency of the bottleneck process by providing increased capacity.
- Find an alternative to the constrained activity and/or resources.
- Redesign the output so that it no longer requires the bottleneck process to be involved in the overall process workflow.

If none of the above remedies are available to the company, it may be that the bottleneck issue will have to be calculated into the output capacity. The process analysis should be monitored to ensure that the bottleneck issue does not increase and that overall efficiency is maximised.

Critical path method

The critical path method of project management is useful for more complex projects than those where process analysis or a Gantt chart would be sufficient. It is still relevant for SMEs and provides graphical analysis of the project stages at a glance.

It is, however, slightly more complicated than the previous methods discussed. Once the project manager has become accustomed to using the critical path method (CPM), however, it is likely to become a preferred method as it deals with time requirements and activity planning of increased complexity with relative ease.

The CPM diagram displays the processes of the project as a network, with the processes represented by nodes, which express the time required for each process. The nodes are then linked by lines to provide a process path from input to output. The inputs and outputs are depicted by a circle. Simply follow the process line and sum the time units on each node. This total is the time required for that process line.

Follow these steps when managing a project using CPM:

- Identify individual activities with the process and give each a unique identifying reference, normally A–Z.
- Find the process line of these activities, ie which activities are a prerequisite for the other activities. The process line must follow a sequential line of events.
- Design the CPM diagram.
- Estimate the time required for each activity and note it against the node displaying the A–Z reference.
- Identify the critical path – this is the path through the network that takes the longest time (as this is the overall time constraint of the project).

The following example will show how to use a CPM in practice. Let's use the example of Bed Co again, though with a slightly more complicated process flow. Each process will have an estimated time requirement for completion – this is the figure in brackets after the process detail:

A = raw materials in to make the bed (six weeks)
B = measurements of the bed required to order the accessories (one week)
C = production of the actual bed (two weeks)
D = finishing of the bed (one week)
E = receipt of accessories from supplier (four weeks).

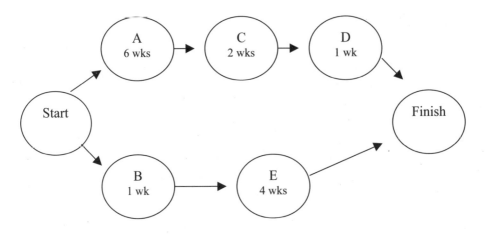

Figure 8.5 Critical path method (Bed Co)

The CPM for this scenario would be as shown in Figure 8.5. As the diagram shows, A–C–D process is sequential and takes 9 weeks, and B–E is sequential and takes 5 weeks.

An aim of the CPM is to ensure that all process lines reach the final output at around the same time. This is to ensure efficient use of working capital. If Bed Co wanted to wait four extra weeks to order the accessories, they would have use of the working capital required for its purchase for an alternative purpose.

Used effectively, CPM will enable the project manager to employ working capital resources to maximum efficiency, while delivering the project on time and to specification.

Remember that these project management tools apply to more than just physical goods; the processes involved can also be equally beneficial to create an idea or concept. Wherever company resources are being allocated to a task, there should be an appropriate method for their costing and appraisal.

Choosing the project manager

As management accounting techniques are often used to provide base data, a member of the accounting team is likely to be called upon to head up a project. A management accountant is likely to have some training in project management and analysis and should therefore be well suited to the role.

In some businesses, where this is not the case, a departmental manager will generally be allocated the role. Project management skills can be learnt and applied through the applications described in this chapter. Above all, a project manager should be an effective communicator. Refer to Chapter 7 on organisational management which has further detail on management styles and where they are appropriate.

It is advisable that the project manager should be somewhat removed from the activities upon which the end result is dependent. Projects often require information and cooperation from several functions of the business and an effective project manager should promote interaction and the flow of information to ensure the project's success.

Don't be alarmed by the terminology and jargon used by project management consultants. The majority of projects can be managed internally without the need for crippling consultancy bills.

IT solutions

Information technology (IT) has made project management very simple. While there is software available that will provide the analysis gained from the above techniques, it is still useful to have an understanding of how they work and the mechanics behind the models. By all means, use an application to manage a project; however, not all projects require this level of detail and Excel can work just as well – provided the project manager has an understanding of the basics of project management as explained in this chapter.

Is there an alternative to project management?

If the company has decided to go ahead with a project, it is recommended that one of the above methods be used to monitor costs and resources effectively. If the project is relatively small and the duration short, then it could be argued that the project could be managed without the use of a formal model. In these cases, a framework should still be used by the project manager, though it could be in a much simpler format of their choosing. The reason for this short-cut would be to save time and company resources on a low-risk project; however, it is no less important to ensure that an alternative and less formal plan takes into account the three basic principles of the project management triangle – time, cost and scope.

Conclusion

Planning a project effectively can save the company time and money and can produce better results to meet objectives. It is advised that any activity, outside day-to-day operations, which calls on company resources over a period of time, should be managed through a project management tool such as those described in this chapter. The most relevant model will depend on the needs of the company and the specific undertaking and the skills of the individuals involved in the project.

Key points to remember

Project management tools can be used for small, short projects and for large-scale projects over many years.

- The use of project management tools will enable management to use resources more effectively than the use of no formal planning.
- The three main project management constraints are displayed using the project management triangle:
  - time;
  - cost;
  - scope.
- Project management models are relevant to small companies, for example:
  - Gantt chart;
  - process analysis;
  - process flow diagram;
  - critical path method.
- Bottlenecks:
  - What is a bottleneck?
  - Process constraint (bottleneck) remedies.
- How to choose an effective project manager.
- IT solutions to aid project management.

9

Information systems

Information is critical for an SME, especially in the modern business world. Market conditions, technological advancements and economic factors can change rapidly, and it is important that a company knows what is happening within the environment in which it operates.

Internally, information is no less important. Efficiency will be improved and profits increased, if effective information systems are in place to communicate relevant information to those who need it within the company. Poor communication is often a reality for many companies that do not have a formal information strategy in place. Information systems needn't be costly or burdensome to produce and, once established, they have proven to deliver tangible results.

An information system will provide a necessary structure or framework upon which data and information can be collected, translated and communicated effectively. In the absence of a suitable framework, information can easily be mislaid or mis-communicated, thus hindering the strategic, management or operational performance of the company.

Data and information

When discussing information systems, it is important to make a clear distinction between data and information. Data is the raw material that is drawn upon to create information. For example, data is a series of competitor prices for a similar product, whereas a chart with comparative analysis carried out on these figures is the information. Information should be meaningful to the person who receives it, whereas data need not be in any precise format or order.

Business areas for information flow

Information should flow around the company from directors to management through to the junior staff members and back up through the ranks. The best information systems in a company are its employees, who have intimate knowledge of what is actually going on, so ensure that an information system includes all staff where possible.

There are three levels of information in the company to consider – strategic, tactical and operational. Each will have a different information need.

Strategic information

Strategic information is distributed or required by shareholders, directors or senior management. Objectives are planned with the use of strategic information, which will be generated from data captured at all levels of the company. The data is then processed into information at a summary level of detail on specific issues relating to the strategic direction and objectives of the company.

Generally, strategic information will be looking at a longer-term view and will be both financial (eg balance sheet) and non-financial (eg competitor analysis). It may rely on more assumptions than operational information, which should be more precise. The type of strategic information required in a company will rely upon the specific strategic objectives set, so use these as the guide as to the desired output of strategic information.

Tactical information

Tactical information is used to employ the resources of the business to ensure that the objectives of the business are met. Once employed, the resources should be analysed and monitored to ensure that they are being used at maximum efficiency. This process would normally be controlled by management and therefore tactical information can also be referred to as management information.

Generated internally, tactical information is concerned with short- and medium-term activities and objectives and is largely based on financial measures, such as profit or cash forecasts and working capital usage statistics. While used by management, data used for tactical information will generally be captured at operational level and compiled routinely by junior-level staff.

Operational information

Operational information is detailed, short term and largely focused on a specific task without the immediate goal of addressing specific objectives. Specific operational tasks will require information to be produced from data captured at this level. Reports will be generated frequently compared with strategic and tactical reporting and will generally be used by junior members of staff. Examples of operational information might include ledger reconciliation, systems error reporting or labour resource information required for payroll purposes.

The three levels of information remain distinct from each other and yet there is a progress link from one stage to the next. For example, a detailed bank reconciliation will be carried out at operational level, to provide management with a summarised bank position by account or currency, which is then summarised into one cash-at-bank figure for strategic purposes. The opposite is also true for information starting at strategic level and becoming more detailed as it filters down to operational requirements.

Case study

An effective information system was essential for Telecoms Co as the company used mainly temporary, transient and external labour to fulfil operating requirements. Information about systems and processes had to be clear and concise and in a format that could be passed on to new people in a way that was understood easily. Strategic information initiated by the director was filtered down through tactical sources to feed to the operational labour resources. While a temporary workforce enabled the flexibility required by the company, it left Telecoms Co without the benefit of capturing the knowledge gained by those working at operational level. The director implemented a series of easy-to-use systems which encouraged those at operational level to provide feedback to the tactical management who then summarised important points and issues for the director at strategic level. The company benefited as a result of this information capture and communication as it had a better understanding of issues at operational level that were having a negative impact on profits, which were then remedied.

The relevance of management accounting to information systems

Information systems are generally created with the view of communicating financial information for the purposes of improved decision making by management. Management accountants provide information to management from the data captured in the finance operation of the company. The architecture of information systems and process management is often created and operated by management accountants as they are often the source of the data.

Management accounting techniques applied to the creation of a formal information system need not be sophisticated – all that is required is a method of capture, a process to turn data into information, determining the users of the information and providing it to those users in a format that they can understand.

Information systems strategy

An information systems strategy is an important place to start as it can be difficult to appreciate the value of good communication or how to go about setting up an effective infrastructure. Think about what information the business currently does not have or how existing information reporting could be improved. Start by setting an objective for each of the following areas that will be impacted upon by an information systems strategy.

Planning

Planning information is that which aids in decision making and resource allocation. The planning and budgeting process requires accurate information from data sourced internally and externally. An objective for planning information might include lead times on the ordering of raw materials or availability of labour resources.

Decision making

Varied data is required for management to make decisions based on accurate information. Decisions should be made by assessing more than one scenario, for example the application of decision tree analysis, which is described in

Chapter 5. This required information may not be generated solely by captured data, but also through assumptions based on research or staff know-how. Information provided for decision making should be clear, concise and summarised, with the ability to gain further detail easily if required.

Controlling

Controlling information also relates to financial factors, such as profitability, and also non-financial information such as physical security of resources or marketing in the environment. For example, an update on the placement of the company's product is controlling information as it enables management to ensure that the agreed placement with a retailer or distributor is being maintained.

Operational management

Detailed data on transactions should be compiled into an operational summary, which is then provided to management so that they can monitor the operational performance and output of the company's resources. This is also the basis for control information.

Performance measurement

Variance analysis is one of the main forms of performance management information, as it measures the difference between actual and planned performance. This information should reflect the company's objectives and subsequent goals to ensure its relevance to management. This information will be a combination of operational management and planning information.

The information objective should be realistic in that it can be generated from existing data. If the data required to provide the desired information is not available, attention should then be given to the methods of data capture used within the company. Data capture methods will be covered in more detail later in this chapter.

Once an objective has been established for each of these key management functions, an information strategy can be created.

Transaction processing system (TPS)

A transaction processing system (TPS) is one of the key areas of information systems upon which a small business should focus. Often, limited resources mean that information systems have not been set up and there is a large element of manual transaction processing, which can be more expensive in the medium to long term. It is important to ensure that all relevant data is captured, while keeping costs down.

A TPS should be created for routine, frequent tasks and should support rather than hinder day-to-day operations. While data is processed and collected in batches before storing, the TPS should only be used when the data is required to be up to date; for example, a batch may only be posted at the end of the business day, which means that a search on an order from the morning will not be found until such point as the batch has been run.

Examples of a TPS include online processing for sales orders, invoice batch processing, order delivery batches or cash receipts. Wherever there is a high level of transactions with a structured routine, a TPS should be implemented.

Figure 9.1 is an example of a batch processing information system that can be implemented in a small business to aid with tasks involving high-volume transactions.

This type of information system not need require an expensive, bespoke software application, which is often cost prohibitive to a small business. The two options are either to design this internally, if the company has the appropriate resources, or to purchase an off-the-shelf package. While the latter will have a generic look and feel, such packages can often be sufficiently tailored to ensure that all data relevant to the specific operations of a company will be captured.

Data sources

Data is generated internally and externally and comes in a wide range of formats. Data can be written or verbal and may or may not be generated with the specific needs of the company in mind. It is up to management to decide what, out of all the possible data sources, is relevant to the company.

Sources of data will, over time, become familiar to those who actively look for and capture data. It may be that you actively look for a piece of data (eg specific research into a competitor) or that data may find you (eg a call from

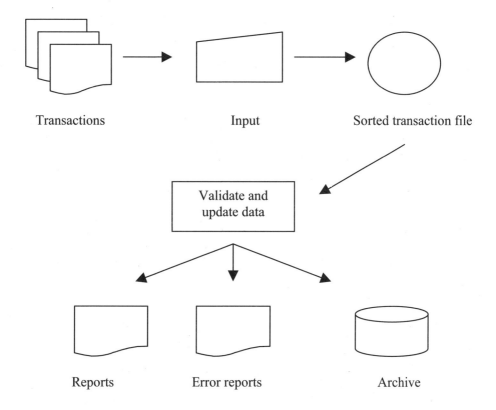

Figure 9.1   Batch processing example

a journalist asking for a response to an activity in the industry). The range of sources is so vast that it would be impossible to list them all, as any activity, group or individual could be a potential data source.

So, how do you know where to look for data that may provide information used to aid the management decisions of the company? Start with a well-planned strategy to find appropriate data sources. For example, if the company operates within the luxury goods sector, a good place to start would be competitors in this market, employees who have worked with luxury goods, publications with a luxury-good focus and customers who may purchase in this market. Once you have established the core sources, widen the net to include other areas such as the wider economic environment. Wider sources may include the mainstream press or external consultants who may have some relevant experience in the area.

When considering data, remember that people are often the best information systems, so be sure to include humans, not just figures, statistics and reports as sources of data.

Data capture

Once the sources have been identified, it is important to be able to capture the data produced. Bear in mind that an effective method of data capture will also include those sources that have yet to be identified.

As information will be the output from the data collected, consider the following issues when setting out to create a method of data capture:

- what type of information is required;
- how frequently that information will be produced;
- what methods are available to process the data into information;
- what resources are available for the data capture.

Meaningful information relies on the integrity and relevance of the underlying data. Not only does data need to be captured, it must remain in its true and pure form, not allowing for any corruption of raw data. Data corruption will ultimately provide information upon which decision making should not be made, thereby rendering it useless and potentially harmful. Ensure that the method of data capture chosen will maintain the integrity of the physical data. The raw data should not be allowed to change form during the process and external influences should not be permitted access to it.

Depending on the type of data, a structured or less formal approach may be taken. Data provided in a report can be captured through a soft copy (electronic format), loaded into a computer and compiled with other relevant data. A conversation may be noted, transcribed and then saved on to a computer for further analysis.

Some methods of data capture require an element of sophistication for their capture, such as electronic data. Some of the data capture methods used for this type of data include:

- Magnetic stripe cards – a plastic card with data recorded on a magnetic stripe, which can then be captured when used in a card reader (eg credit cards).

- Smart cards – a plastic card containing a microprocessor chip which has memory and processing capabilities.
- Bar codes – a series of thick and thin stripes aligned and spaced to provide a unique fingerprint, with which to identify specific values or data.
- Scanner – if data has been provided in hard copy (eg paper), it can be scanned and entered into a computer. The content of the document or file will be read and formatted to provide this data in a more user-friendly format.

The following are all communication tools which should be used in conjunction with the methods of data capture:

- meetings;
- telephone conversations;
- personal conversations (unstructured);
- formal presentations;
- reports and memorandums;
- e-mail and letters.

The method(s) chosen for a specific company should be practical, based on the availability of resources, and should provide relevant data in a secure format which is then easily processed into quality information.

Knowledge management

When searching for data sources and deciding on a data capture method, remember that some of the best knowledge will be that already held by those within the company. This isn't always easy to access, as those who have the required knowledge may not know it is required and may not even know the value of the knowledge they possess.

It could also be the case that employees wish to retain data for their own use. The company should be aware of knowledge that is available and may need to incentivise employees to share the knowledge that they have gained. Generally, an employee contract should state that knowledge gained during the course of employment is the right of the company; however, this can be difficult to enforce in practice.

Many large companies are aware of this issue and aim to collect, store and use the knowledge already captured by their own resources. Small companies should also employ a method of knowledge management, as the concept is no less relevant to them than to larger companies. One method of knowledge management is to hold brainstorming activities, where participants are encouraged to provide their ideas on a specific topic, which are designed to generate a wide range of views and opinions. The output should be documented electronically for future reference.

Other 'knowledge items' may be extracted by filling out a form on a specific subject, requiring financial data such as times, dates, quantities, customer profiles etc. A common example of this is for selected staff to visit a trade show. Staff members who visit a trade show would be asked to compile a list of competitor or complementary products along with relevant data such as prices, product placement, product quality or packaging. This information would be passed on to other employees for their knowledge, and retained on file for future use. Not all data will be quantifiable, which is why communication is so important to knowledge management. However, knowledge should be available for future users, where possible, so it is important to document the thoughts and feelings of employees where possible.

An effective knowledge management system will not only capture and store data, it will also distribute it among colleagues to promote innovation and initiatives to be discussed. This is a trend worldwide with large companies, but can work just as well with a small team environment where small ideas or experiences can grow into a workable operating strategy. Communicating knowledge can also provide information to others to prevent the same mistakes being made or provide advice on how to improve a process.

Case study

AdCo recognised that its employees' experiences with clients were generating some very interesting scenarios. The company operated in groups, which meant that if one group had an experience, a member in another group might not benefit from the experience of the other group. Rather than change their group structure, the directors created an 'experience board'. This was simply a Word document saved on the shared network. When an employee had an interesting, relevant business experience, he or she would post details of the situation and outcome on the board. Colleagues could then access the document, perform a search on key words and hopefully benefit from the experience. This is a common concept in larger companies, which generally use an intranet for the sharing of information and ideas. A shared Word document works just as well for a small company.

Using information systems competitively

A company can improve its level of competitiveness with the effective use of information systems. Business objectives at a strategic and management level can be affected positively with information systems that are created at an operational level. The company should see the use of information systems as integral to its communication of objectives around the company.

Once internal communications are operating effectively, information systems can be used externally to become a competitive advantage for the company. Consider three external stakeholders of the business as to how this theory may work in practice.

Customers

Customers provide information on special deals, new products or other details that might entice them to purchase or continue to purchase your product. Providing a mechanism, such as a website, to enable customers to access information about your product easily can give a competitive advantage over a company that does not have a web presence or whose website is not user-friendly.

Suppliers

An efficient information system can be established for comparative analysis on supplier pricing, thus enabling the company to buy at the best price, influencing power over the supplier.

New entrants

Information regarding customer contracts and costs of switching to a different supplier could prevent a new entrant from entering the market. Also, publishing information on the expense of setting up operations could act as a deterrent for those new companies with insufficient working capital.

Consider the external environment and ensure that your information systems provide an efficient way to communicate and provide access to your company and its products.

Characteristics of good information

Using data to produce information for the company is not, in itself, enough. The information must be good quality information which is valuable to the people who will use it.

A useful acronym for the characteristics of good information is QUALITY. This is a helpful guide to remember the merits of good information and recognise any problems or weaknesses with the type or flow of information within the company or wider environment.

Quantitative and qualitative

Information should be able to be quantified or understood in terms of financial analysis, but also provide information on non-financial data such as quality or other less tangible factors.

User-targeted

The style or format of information should always be prepared with the user's requirements in mind. The presenter of the information should also consider the background of the user. For example, presenting a set of accounts would provide different supporting information if the user was an accountant or an individual with no financial experience.

Accurate

Information should be reliable and the user should have absolute confidence in the integrity of its contents. If one piece of information has been exposed with errors, all other information produced from that information system or data source will be called into question.

Labelled

Make sure the user knows what information he or she is reading by using clear labels for different information. For example, a common mistake is to provide a coloured line chart in black and white. In this case the lines all look the same colour, rendering it useless unless it is sufficiently labelled.

Informative

It might sound obvious, but ensure that the information is actually providing the user with information. Do not provide a report containing raw data that has not been sufficiently analysed or formatted to produce the desired level of information. It could be that while 'information' might be understood by one person, the user may find it difficult to interpret.

Timely

Ensure that information is processed and presented to the user within an efficient timeframe, which is relevant to the decision-making process. Information can often be rendered useless if it is too late to impact on any managerial or strategic decisions.

Yield

The information should provide the user with the required amount of information. Don't overload the user with detail that might be irrelevant for the purpose, and conversely, ensure that a sufficient amount information is provided without leaving any gaps.

Social change and ethics

Business trends follow that of the wider social community – and quite often the opposite is true. Society now expects information at the touch of a button. We feel the need – and often the right – to be able to access immediately any piece of information we feel is necessary to our tasks. We have become demanding in terms of information, while technology has been driven to keep up with these ever-increasing demands.

Businesses have no choice but to reflect this increasing demand for information. If they don't, they will be left behind. The stronger the demand for a wider range of information, the closer business and society step towards ethical boundaries of disclosure. The demand for information does not immediately equate to the right to receive or deliver that information. There is a point where ethics will draw a line at the changing social demand for information – though this constraint in itself is constantly being tested.

While ethics should be considered in all areas of business, information systems are a particularly relevant area for the consideration and application of a policy towards ethics. Customer and employee privacy must be considered when developing an information system and its data requirements and informational outputs. Both parties have a right to control or limit information given (or taken) by a company, regardless of its use.

Be clear about the rights and obligations of the company when developing a data capture method and information distribution system to ensure that ethical considerations are not breached.

Conclusion

An effective information system is essential to an SME to aid strategic decisions and to close communication gaps between the strategic, management and operational levels of the company. Through an efficient system, the essential data can be captured, which will then be developed into information upon which management can base decisions with the aim of fulfilling the company's full potential.

When creating an information system, it can be easy to focus on the information technology element. Don't forget about the best information systems in a company – the people who work there. Data, information and its effective communication is essential to a small business that wants to maximise its profits.

Key points to remember

- Information systems help management discover and retain knowledge about the external environment in which they operate.
- Internal information will be better captured and communicated with the use of an effective information system.
- Data and information – clear distinction between the two terms for the purposes of information systems:
    - Data is the raw material upon which information is created.
    - Information is the summary of data which is read by the user.
- There are three levels of information in a company:
    - strategic – medium to long term and high level;
    - tactical – medium term and mid level;
    - operational – short term and low level.
- An information systems strategy should start with objectives from the following business areas:
    - planning;
    - decision making;
    - controlling;
    - operational management;
    - performance management.
- A transaction processing system (TPS) should be adopted by the company to capture data and provide information output. A TPS is especially useful for batch processing activities.
- Data sources should be reviewed for the company. Ensure that all relevant data is captured by identifying all potential sources of data.
- Data capture methods can include electronic, such as bar codes and scanners, or other methods, such as meetings and presentations.
- Knowledge management is the capture, sorting and communication of knowledge gained by a group or individuals to benefit other groups of individuals. Small companies should set up a form of shared document to benefit from each other's experiences.
- Use information systems competitively to obtain information about customers, suppliers, existing competitors and new entrants to the market.
- Good information can be characterised by the QUALITY acronym:
    - Q – Quantitative and qualitative
    - U – User-targeted
    - A – Accurate

- – L – Labelled
- – I – Informative
- – T – Timely
- – Y – Yield.
- Social change and ethics should be considered when collecting and communicating information relating to third parties.

10

Contract law

Contracts are everywhere in business. We all make contracts every day, whether in written or verbal format. A small business owner/manager should understand and be able to navigate a basic business contract to ensure that the business is not unnecessarily exposed.

Contracts are no less important in an SME than in a large multinational, sometimes more so as small businesses have little defence and mistakes can be costly to the business. Also, it is unusual for a small business to be able to afford a dedicated legal resource, so this task normally falls to the manager or the accountant.

It is not a difficult area to grasp and once the basic terminology has been learnt, contract negotiation will become second nature. This knowledge may save the company – both financially and in terms of reputation.

Note that this chapter draws upon the concepts of UK contract law.

The relevance of management accounting to contract law

Unlike the other chapters in this book, there are no specific management accounting techniques that can be applied to contract law in terms of execution or analysis of a task or area of the business. Contract law is a standalone subject and we will cover the same detail and information as those looking at the topic from outside the management accounting focus. However, contract law is linked with the financial operations and performance of the company and the impact of a contract should always be considered when negotiating or agreeing to the terms and conditions of a third party.

Beware legalese (jargon)

Contracts aren't always plain speaking and this can confuse people who aren't used to the jargon that lawyers inevitably use.

Case study

A recent client of mine was presented with a contract. He didn't read or sufficiently understand the fine print of every clause in the 12-page contract, but thought it was just standard terms and conditions, so signed it anyway. The contract was with a supplier to buy raw materials to make a new product for the company. The purchase price had been negotiated and was considered to be a good price by management and would therefore provide the company with a product of improved profitability. In the small print, however, was a cleverly worded minimum order quantity clause, which stated that should 100,000 units not be purchased within the first six months, these must be paid for whether ordered or not. The company had a requirement for only 50,000 units and therefore found itself having to buy materials it didn't need. The result was a loss-making product and angry shareholders.

Not all contracts are seeking to confuse the reader, however. Some are easy to understand and navigate and yet it is still important to understand what constitutes a contract and to know exactly what you are committing the company to.

In this chapter we will cover the basics of understanding a contract through legal principles and how to cut through confusing terminology.

Contract law – basic principles

A contract is an exchange of promises between parties, which is considered legally binding. Sometimes a contract must be in writing to be legally binding; more often though, a verbal contract is sufficient.

It is important to know how a contract actually forms, as well as what format it must take to be legally binding. There are three elements to the formation of a contract:

1. offer and acceptance;
2. consideration;
3. intention to create a legal obligation.

Let's look at each of these essential elements of a contract in turn.

Offer and acceptance

The most important feature of a contract is offer and acceptance, which requires one party to make an offer for a specific transaction, which is then accepted by another party. A contract will be formed when each party can provide evidence that they will conduct the transaction with the intention of fulfilling their obligations, as defined by a reasonable person.

Offer and acceptance does not always need to be expressed orally or in writing. A contract may also be implied and therefore not be required to be in writing or to be signed. For example, if you phone a painter and ask him to visit your office to paint a new sign outside your building, you are then entering into a contract. He comes to the office and performs the job as required. You are required by law to pay the painter his fee for the work as it was 'implied' that you would do so when asking him to do the work. If you do not pay the painter his fee, you are in breach of contract despite no paper having been signed.

Consideration

The concept of consideration is that each party must provide to the other contractual parties something of perceived value. This can be an area of contention as the perception of value can differ between parties and therefore it is very important that any issues of consideration, namely payment, be agreed and carefully recorded in sufficient detail as part of the body of the contract.

This is a common area for mistakes and ambiguity. If in doubt, include more detail than less to avoid misinterpretation of the consideration due to each party.

There are three rules that control consideration:

1. Consideration must be sufficient, but need not be adequate. A contract to purchase office equipment can be satisfied with the amount of £1 stated as consideration provided that each party has read and understands the contractual obligation.
2. Consideration must be present or future value and, therefore, must not be from the past. For example, when entering into a contract to supply goods to a customer, past payment or credits cannot be carried forward into the contract.
3. Consideration must move from the party who is making the promise of payment. If there are several parties to the contract, the rule that must be satisfied is that the consideration must move from the party who is making the promise – it needn't travel to the party to whom the goods or services are being delivered. For example, if A Ltd provides window cleaning to B Ltd, they are allowed to be paid by B Ltd's parent company C Ltd. The payment needn't be paid directly from B Ltd; however, the initial act must come from A Ltd and therefore the reciprocal consideration must return to this party.

'Estoppel' is a term often linked with consideration. It is an equitable measure that provides for the creation of legal obligations if a party has given another an assurance and the other has relied on this assurance to his or her detriment. This can be called upon when consideration has failed to be passed.

Intention to create a legal obligation

There is an assumption in contract law that if parties enter into a contract, their intention is to create a legal obligation. This is easily argued in terms of a business meeting with negotiations surrounding an existing or future transaction; however, if there is a situation whereby there is no intention to enter into a legally binding contract, this should be clearly stated. Without stating an intent to remain free from legal obligation, you may become a party to a contract to which you do not wish to be bound. As with all areas of contract law, make your true intentions known to all relevant parties.

Case study

Telecoms Co had a meeting with a supplier. It was considered a good meeting by both parties as they both found areas where they could work together to increase efficiency and, in Telecoms Co's case, growth. There were a lot of positive comments and the meeting ended with handshakes all round. When the director of Telecoms Co said 'that all sounds great' at the end of the meeting, he meant 'let's have further discussions and see how things go', whereas the supplier took it to mean 'let's start trading'. The misunderstanding wasn't realised until Telecoms Co received their first invoice from the supplier a week later. At this point, clarity was achieved, though Telecoms Co and the supplier had to come to an agreement about the work provided as a result of miscommunication.

Format – does a contract have to be in writing?

We've all heard the saying 'not worth the paper it's written on', but how do we know if a contract is actually a contract and when does a contract have to be in writing? As we saw in the section on offer and acceptance, a contract needn't be in writing for it to be legally binding. There are, however, some contracts that must be in writing to allow parties to use the law as remedial action should another party not fulfil an obligation.

Guarantees and the sale and purchase of land are among contracts that must be in writing. The law does not require many operational business contracts to be in writing; however, it makes good business sense to enter into a formal written contract for all material agreements to which the company is a party. The company should reduce its exposure wherever possible through the use of formal, written contracts, even if the form taken is a few clear notes on a page, which is then signed by the authorised parties.

A note on who can sign contracts. Generally, contracts should only be signed by an individual who is authorised to do so by the company. A director or senior manager is normally the only level of staff who can sign on behalf of the company. This power should be stated in the employee contract of each individual. If signatory power is in doubt, ask and confirm that the person signing has the power to do so.

Written contracts that may be entered into should include:

- Employment contracts detailing full remuneration package and entitlements along with any regulations on company policy.
- Freelance labour should also be contractual and detail rate per day and hour.
- Leases such as building, office equipment, motor vehicle.
- Customer and supplier contracts should note all issues specific to that party, such as payment terms, product specification, minimum orders and delivery agreements.
- Shareholder agreements should detail the number of shares and associated consideration.

Considering contract law in the practical terms of a small business, it is not essential to enter into a contract with all of the stakeholders in your business. A comprehensive list of stakeholders is given in Chapter 1. For example, you do not need to sign a contract when you purchase stationery; however, if you buy items on credit, there will often be a set of terms and conditions either on a website or on the back of an invoice. Upon order and receipt of these goods you are entering into the terms of the supplier and that is a contract.

Components of a contract

It is now important to understand the component parts of a contract and how you can have a positive impact on how a contract can affect your business. The terms of a contract are not always set in stone by the other party and are quite often open to negotiation. Once the terms have been agreed by the parties, they will form the body of the contract. So, what exactly is a term of a contract?

Term

A term of a contract is a statement of fact used by a party to induce another party to enter into a legally binding agreement. The term must be guaranteed by the party making the statement and must be supported by factual evidence that can be presented if required to do so.

Terms can be changed after the contract is signed, but must be done through a written amendment to the original contract, the new terms of which must be agreed by all parties. The detail of this amendment is normally included as a schedule or addendum to the original contract and should clearly cite which clause, or part-clause, it replaces.

Contracts may also include 'implied' terms. To argue the inclusion of an implied term, it must pass a reasonableness test as set down by previous case law. The test of an implied term is that it must be necessary, consistent and obvious to, and in the context of, the contract. The term must also be said using clear language and expression.

Representation

A representation is different from a term. A representation is a statement of fact which is made by one party with the aim of persuading and encouraging another party to enter into a contract. Unlike a term, the statement is not guaranteed by the party who made the contract and therefore it is not deemed to be a term of a contract. Therefore, if a representation is not upheld it does not breach the contract. However, if a party does not adhere to a representation, the other party may be able to label the breach a misrepresentation and thereby have other remedies available to them.

Completeness

If a contract is deemed to be incomplete or uncertain, an agreement has not taken place between the parties in the eyes of the law. Ensure that all ambiguity over terms has been addressed and, should all parties wish to enter into a legal contract, make this intention clear at the end of the contract through signing, dating, and witnessing if deemed necessary.

Remedy

A remedy may be available to a party of a contract who feels, and can prove, that they have been the victim of another party who has failed to meet the terms of the contract. Should it be proved that a party has failed to meet his or her terms of the contract, it is considered that the contract has been breached. Upon breach, the contract can be cancelled by the injured party and a remedy may be given to the party to whom the breach occurred.

The most common remedy for breach of contract is damages, which are paid by the party who committed the breach of the terms of the contract to the other party(ies) of the contract, where appropriate. There are three common types of damages:

- Nominal damages – a token sum of money paid to establish a precedent in law or where the breach is a matter of principle.
- Compensatory damages – payment of a sufficient amount by the guilty party to ensure that the innocent party is not out of pocket through and as a result of the actions of the guilty party. A profit should never be seen to be made through claiming compensatory damages as the payment should ensure that the innocent party is as they would have been had the contract remained in place and had operated in line with its terms.
- Punitive damages – awarded to punish the guilty party and not just restore the innocent party back to the normal trading position as with the case of compensatory damages. The actions of the guilty party would normally be quite exceptional in these cases as the law would normally offer compensatory damages only.

Subject to contract

In business, one often finds the term 'subject to contract' on legal documents. When this term is used, it means that the parties have made an indication that they may wish to enter into a contract should terms be agreed. Depending on the type of transaction, there are varying levels of actions required by parties to be classed as subject to contract.

These range from an agreement to enter into discussions about a deal, which will not be concluded until the final contract has been drawn up and signed, to a situation where the parties are immediately bound to a deal as they have clearly stated their intent to enter into an agreement, whereby the terms of the contract will not differ from those presently agreed.

Again, this is an area where one should be careful about the language used in negotiations. Only be bound to a contract that you have agreed to enter into without coercion.

Contract law and the SME

So, now you know what a contract is, how to put one together and understand the basic terminology surrounding contract law. There should be no need to seek out expensive legal advice for contracts; however, if you are uncertain, it is better playing it safe than sorry. Getting a contract wrong can be an expensive lesson to learn.

Beware of the language used by other parties, as they may be looking to enter into a legal arrangement to which you do not wish to commit. Conversely, if you do wish to form a contract with another party, ensure that this is also their intention, and that you make clear your wishes to do so.

If in doubt, put it in. There's no point complaining about a customer not paying for carriage of goods when it was not included in the contract. A contract isn't just for the large, expensive issues – it is your chance to include all of the details that you feel are relevant to the contract and to the ongoing working relationship between the parties.

Conclusion

Getting a contract right at the beginning can help to keep relationships on track. A contract can act as an independent arbiter when the going gets tough and one of the parties may wish to alter the arrangements. Being able to fall back on a well-executed contract is a big advantage and contract law should be approached as an essential tool for any SME owner and/or manager.

Key points to remember

- Contracts are everywhere in business and are entered into every day.
- Beware legalese (jargon). Don't be too proud to ask for clarification on a confusing clause in a contract.
- The basic principles of contract law are:
  - offer and acceptance;
  - consideration;
  - intention to create a legal obligation.
- A contract doesn't have to be in writing for it to be upheld by the law.

- Make sure the person who is signing the contract on behalf of each party is authorised to do so, both by their employer and in the eyes of the law.
- Components of a contract:
  - term;
  - representation;
  - completeness;
  - remedy and damages including:
    - nominal
    - compensatory
    - punitive.
- 'Subject to contract' can be ambiguous depending on the agreements and indications surrounding the specific issue, so be certain what your obligations are.

3

Corporate finance

11

Corporate finance for small businesses

Corporate finance for small business focuses on the structure of the company and providing sufficient working capital for the company to maximise its profits. It also provides tools for expansion or an exit. The SME owner/manager need not have an in-depth working knowledge of complex market hypotheses and investment appraisal techniques, but he or she should have an awareness of what resources are available to the business and how they could be applied to improve performance.

What is corporate finance?

The nature of corporate finance is to maximise the financial wealth of companies and their shareholders. The perception of the methods used by financiers to achieve this aim can be rather intimidating. Mention corporate finance to small business owners and they will probably feel that it is not something that would be appropriate to the size or complexity of their business. This is wrong – corporate finance is just that – finance for corporate entities, and that means small companies just as much as large multinationals.

Not all corporate finance techniques and applications will be relevant, however. For the purposes of this chapter, we will assume that a small business is a private, limited company, which is not part of a group and therefore any public company activities are not relevant and will be excluded from our analysis.

Corporate finance provides a structure in which a company can have access to a variety of techniques outside its normal operating environment. Some relevant benefits to the small business would include:

- access to working capital (sources of finance);
- better understanding of the value of the existing business;
- providing the company with the best-fit capital structure;
- approaches to an acquisition, merger or trade sale;
- shareholder strategy and management;
- risk management.

Let's look at each of these points in turn as they are all relevant to the small business owner/manager who is looking to maximise the potential in and from his or her business.

Sources of finance

There will come a time in the life of the company, whether at start-up or growth phase, when you will need to think about how you are going to finance the business and its strategic objectives. Often companies require working capital early in the process of setting up a company; however, this is not always the case if a business can generate immediate working capital through supplier and/or customer terms or some other mechanism.

Establish the timing and value of the working capital requirement. If it is seed capital that is required (investment at start-up phase), this data should be included in your business plan. If the finance requirement is to enable growth or support a period of cash constraint, a separate analysis should be generated by management showing the effect on the profitability and assets of the business. This report should also include detail of any dilution of existing share capital and its effect on shareholders.

Let's look at two types of finance for the business – seed capital and operating capital.

Seed capital

This is the money (or assets) required to turn the business idea or concept into an operating business. The capital may be used to produce a sample run of your product, for initial marketing or premises or even to actively launch the company. This expenditure will cover the set-up phase of your business.

Operating capital

Once you have set up your business, you may need to have an investment of operating capital to cover expenditure until such point as revenues can generate a profit and subsequent cash surplus. The term of this cash (or asset) requirement will depend on your business and its success in the market.

Case study

For Telecoms Co, cash wasn't a priority to set up the company. Initially it was all about contacts and putting in place optimal terms with customers and suppliers to roll out a seamless working capital cycle, ie the supplier was paid after the customer receipt was received. Very little working capital was required – or so the director thought. Two issues that would necessitate a review of this plan soon became apparent. First, suppliers offered a cheaper rate if Telecoms Co could prepay for certain services. The director calculated that the additional profit gained would exceed the cost of the borrowed capital, and was worth the risk of borrowing.

Second, customers were lagging in payment and meanwhile suppliers were threatening to stop service if they weren't paid on time. In an industry where prompt payment is the norm, this was an unexpected problem for Telecoms Co. The director soon realised that he would have to bridge the working capital gap for a two-week period while he waited for customer receipts. While the cost of this capital reduced his overall profit, it was essential to inject working capital to ensure the ongoing operations of the business.

Equity vs loan capital

There are two main approaches to raising either seed or operating finance – equity or loan capital. A financier can provide cash or business assets in exchange for a shareholding (equity) in your company. Generally this will be a percentage of ordinary shares based on an agreed valuation of the business. A shareholding will normally bring with it some element of control or management input from the financier or his or her delegate, such as a board seat.

A loan is an amount of cash (or asset) provided to the business by a lender, with a view that the business will repay the capital with an interest premium. A business loan can take many forms and can be flexible depending on the needs and financial position of the business.

Start-up companies often prefer a loan option for seed and early operational capital rather than equity as the valuation of an early-stage company is likely to be low – quite often much lower than the business owner would care to admit. The risk for an investor is much higher and therefore they require the reward to be higher and reflect the level of risk and financial exposure. While loan finance is often more expensive to the business in terms of working capital than equity, it is often preferable to parting with a high percentage of equity from the company's infancy.

Sources of capital available to small businesses

Banks

Many banks will offer start-up business loans to companies that they perceive as relatively low risk and that have assets against which a loan can be secured. If the company has insufficient assets, they will look to the personal assets of directors who will be expected to provide a personal guarantee against the value of the loan. Banks will also provide other forms of credit, including overdrafts, which can be a useful bridging tool, though this can often be an expensive source of finance. It is very rare that banks will require (or want) equity in a company. Make sure that you are aware of the bank fees involved, as there is often an arrangement fee and quite often a monitoring fee. The assorted fees charged can quickly add up, so ensure that all costs are factored into the budget and cashflow forecast in line with when they are due to be paid.

Friends and family

Tread carefully! While borrowing from friends and family can be a cheap source of capital, there are personal relationships at risk if the business venture doesn't go according to plan. Ensure that the people who are offering the investment are fully aware of the business plan and associated risks involved in the venture. This capital may come in pure cash or asset form, or equity may be part of the deal. It is up to the parties involved to determine the specific details of the arrangement. From experience, try to keep the deal as close to market rates as possible as this will allow the business to register the appropriate cost, which will negate any potential argument from the lender – now or in the future.

Business angels

While usually a high net worth individual, business angels can sometimes form a consortium for lending to, or investing in, small companies. This can be a beneficial option as business angels often expect (and want) to invest their time and experience as well as their money. Business angels are normally found through word of mouth or business networks, so if this is a route you are looking to investigate, start the process earlier as there are often longer lead times for a business angel to review and provide feedback than a larger institution such as a bank.

Government grants

The government promotes small business. They like the idea that businesses are starting up throughout the UK to provide them with more taxes and to reduce the unemployment rate. They encourage small businesses with financial and information-based support where they can, and part of this initiative is government grants. You will need to contact the Department for Business, Enterprise and Regulatory Reform in the first instance and they will point you in the right direction depending on your business requirement. Make sure you read the fine print and that you meet the initial and ongoing criteria as stated.

Own cash reserves

Often the cheapest way of starting up and supporting a new business is to use your own savings. One exception to this rule would be if your personal savings are earning a very high return in interest payments, which outweighs the cost of borrowing from another source.

Credit cards

I am constantly amazed by the number of people using credit cards to bridge a cashflow deficit in their business. Use this as a last resort and only if the need is short-term, ie less than three months, and if you are certain that a fixed, identified cash inflow will be secured by the business within that timeframe. Credit cards are expensive and overexposure can lead to a very fast downward spiral.

Regardless of the source of finance chosen for the company, ensure that it will be able to repay interest, as and when it falls due, from the retained profits of the business. Paying interest from the capital originally invested can result in a trading position that is untenable for anything other than the short term.

Capital structure

The capital structure of a small company is unlikely to be complicated. Small, private companies will generally derive their capital from a combination of loan capital and equity. A loan is money or other assets borrowed from a party in return for interest payments and repayment of the capital at a specified time. Equity is an investment from a third party in exchange for shares in the company, thus creating a shareholder.

As we saw at the beginning of the chapter, the decision over whether to fund the business using loan or equity finance is dependent upon the assets of the company, its trading performance and requirements, and the objectives of the shareholders. When the capital structure is formed, it is important to report on any significant changes as this is likely to have an impact on the value of the business.

Cost of capital

Borrowing money or assets will result in a cost to the business. The total capital requirement should be based on financial analysis of the identified need for the funding, such as project finance or bridging a working capital gap. If a loan is taken out, management should factor all costs of borrowing into the financial planning for the business, such as rate of interest, timing of interest and capital repayments, late fees and over-borrowing fees (ie if you have arranged to borrow £100 and you actually borrow £110, the extra £10 could be charged at a higher rate than the agreed £100).

If the capital is generated through equity, a full analysis of its impact on shareholders and their percentage ownership should be carried out.

Capital is essential at some stage for all businesses to expand and grow. Tread carefully when making decisions on borrowing and take your time to weigh up the risks and return of each proposal, as these could be relationships that last for the life of your business.

Mergers and acquisitions

Not all small businesses will benefit from merger and acquisition (M&A) activities; however, as it is an option available to any legal corporate entity, the owner/manager should be aware of its applications. Potential applications of M&A activity for a small, private business include improved sales or profits, a reduction in operating costs, growth through acquisition or an exit strategy.

Improve sales or profits

An increase in market share and subsequent turnover may be the objective from a merger or acquisition. Note that an increase in turnover may not necessarily bring with it an increase in profits. While there are efficiencies to be made by M&A, such as economies of scale, the target company may not be profitable and can therefore reduce overall profits of the newly formed group. This is generally a short-term problem until such time as the operational efficiencies are identified and removed. Thorough due diligence should be carried out to ensure that the target company will ultimately provide profits and not just turnover, if profits are also the objective.

Reduce operating costs

A merger of companies will often be motivated by the potential of economies of scale which enable the company to buy for less, as it will generally be buying more units. The bargaining power of the supplier should be reduced when the company begins ordering larger quantities, resulting in a lower purchase price and often improved service from suppliers. It is also likely that duplication in resource will be found from a merger of two legal entities, thus creating an unnecessary overlap – most often in the labour resource. Reducing total labour resource can be an efficient way to reduce operating costs.

Growth through acquisition

When a business has grown organically to a level where management feel that further growth would either not be possible or would involve too much risk, the purchase of a competitor can often provide a greater market share and associated profits. An acquisition could also be made of a company which offers a complementary product or a supplier, thus growing the company while providing cost-saving benefits.

Exit strategy

Exit through the sale of a small business can often be the objective for the owners and thus M&A options should be investigated. A large proportion of SME trade sales are made to their competitors, though other potential acquirers could be private or institutional investors or a management team established from inside or outside the business. Exit strategies will be covered in more detail in Chapter 12.

Shareholder strategy

An SME should have a strategy to manage their shareholders as they are an important stakeholder in the business. Their objectives must be considered, as the statutory directors have a fiduciary duty to increase shareholders' wealth. Ideally a company culture and operational structure will provide goal congruence, though this duty to the shareholders should be the priority if there is ever conflict.

While increasing shareholder wealth through the increase in company value should remain the focus of director and therefore management activities, shareholders' actual powers are quite limited. There is clearly an exception in situations where the shareholder is also a director.

A shareholder who does not hold a board position does not have any right to inspect company accounts, budgets or internal communications, such as letters and memos. They have the right to request this information, though the directors can decide to refuse it – however, politically, this should be based on a very good reason so as not to create tension in the capital structure of the company.

Dividend policy

A shareholder has invested capital into the company as an investment and will expect a certain return on that investment. This will have been agreed at the time of investment. The company must ensure that it can satisfy these requirements. The return on shareholder equity takes the form of dividends, as well as the increase in capital value realised upon exit. Dividends are distributed from the retained profits of the company to the shareholders on a pro rata basis. For example, if a shareholder has 8 per cent of the company, he can expect to receive 8 per cent of the dividend pool.

The directors decide on the amount of the dividend pool, thus requiring the need for an established dividend policy. The dividend policy will guide the directors as to how they approach the use of retained profits. Shareholders will often enquire as to the dividend policy before investing as they may be less inclined to invest in a company that intends to have no dividend pool for five years. In this case, the shareholder could only expect an increase in the value of the shares, without receipt of cash through dividends during this time. In theory, however, the value of shares should be greater than had retained profits been paid out in dividends as they were used to grow the business which in turn should increase its value.

The dividend policy may create a conflict between the two parties as goal congruence is not achieved. Generally, shareholders seek dividends and directors aim to use retained profits for reinvestment into the company. The key is to adopt a dividend policy as part of the overall shareholder policy early in the life of the company. Any deviation from this should be accompanied by a formal business proposal for an alternative use of the retained profits.

Case study

Design Co was set up many years ago by two directors. Over the years, their management input has decreased yet they have retained 100 per cent shareholding between them. The current management of the company wish to expand the business as they see opportunities abroad which they believe will increase profits. To enable this growth, management need to use the retained profits for reinvestment. The shareholders, however, wish the company to continue to pay the retained profits out in dividends, resulting in cash payments to themselves. This lack of goal congruence has frustrated management; however, the shareholders (who are also directors) have final say over the dividend policy, so it is likely that management will continue to experience frustration if they continue to push for expansion requiring retained profits.

Risk and return

Entering into an investment opportunity or contract with an existing customer or supplier requires thorough analysis to ensure that it will be the best use of the resources of the company, thereby maximising the wealth of the shareholders.

A key part of this decision is a risk and return analysis. The simple equation is: how profitable is the venture (reward) against the potential exposure (risk) to the company? The basic principle of corporate finance is that risk should be equal to the reward. Therefore, a high-risk project should expect to gain greater profits and returns than normal day-to-day operations of a company as the latter are more likely to be planned and based on historic data, thus reducing the perceived risk.

A full description of the management accounting techniques, namely discounted cashflow and decision tree analysis, which can be used for investment analysis are covered in more detail in Chapter 5.

Risk management

For a company to operate to achieve its strategic, tactical and operational objectives, it will inevitably adopt an element of risk. The risk factor should determine the level of reward. The risk element will deter many new entrants from the industry, while maintaining an element of competitiveness between existing companies.

The risk taken by a company should be calculated as much as possible, with a focus on the threat to the resources of the company. Where it is acknowledged that risk must be adopted, a risk management process should be implemented to better understand the exposure of the company's assets and resources.

The application of a risk management strategy is also designed to maximise potential from opportunities and convey the confidence of management to shareholders and other relevant stakeholders. It should also reduce management resource spent on managing uncalculated or unforeseen exposure of resources. When a strategy has been agreed, it can be beneficial to communicate this to the relevant parties to enable the above factors to be recognised.

There is a four-step process to risk management – identify, assess, prioritise and control risk.

Identify

It is essential to recognise where a risk may currently exist or where a potential risk may occur in the future. The task of identifying risks should cover the entire company and its processes from strategic to operational levels. An effective risk management system should lead management to the exact point of risk and provide details of its origin and composition.

Assess

Before risk is knowingly adopted, a thorough examination of the potential risks and their financial impact on the company should be carried out. There will be risks that occur that were not calculated. These unforeseen risks, once identified, should be quantified to establish their impact on the reward and objectives.

Prioritise

Risk management allows risks to be classified by their impact on the company and its financial performance. Once identified, a ranking system should be applied to risks based on the assessment of their financial impact. Steps towards management of each identified risk should be carried out based on the ranking prioritisation profile.

Control

Risks will be inevitable and sometimes it will not be possible to remove them from the operational process. Controlled risks become reduced risks. Control should aid management decisions and the ability to apply resources effectively. The threat from risk can be reduced by the introduction of enhanced operational controls, such as reporting, communication and analysis between all relevant parties. Refer to Chapter 9 on information systems for details of how to use communication as a control mechanism.

Once a risk management strategy and process has been implemented it should be monitored, with results communicated where relevant, to ensure that the exposure of the company's resources is kept to a minimum. This approach should also be targeted towards protecting the expected reward.

Advisers – when you need them and what to expect

Corporate finance is an incredibly specialised field. When financiers start training at basic level they normally already have an accounting or legal qualification under their belt, to which more years of training and work experience are added. Advisers in this field have developed the skills and experience necessary to advise on decisions worth hundreds of millions of pounds – and as a result they don't come cheap.

Most of the corporate finance areas covered in this chapter could be carried out without the need for employing the services of an adviser. However, should the owners of an SME wish to sell, expand through external investment or take their business public, it would be advisable to use a corporate finance adviser who has up-to-date knowledge of the market in which the company operates and the regulations that apply. Corporate finance advisers should be regulated by the Financial Services Authority (FSA).

A tip for small businesses is that some corporate financiers may provide the required service for a success-dependent fee. This can be of great peace of mind to a small business owner, as many corporate finance transactions started do not complete, owing to a range of issues such as failed due diligence or a party withdrawing from the process.

Conclusion

Corporate finance applies just as significantly to the SME as to larger, public companies. There are many options available to the owners and directors of a small business to ensure that the company is reaching its operating and growth potential.

Proceed with caution, however, as substantial resources could be wasted if your research and business planning have not been carried out meticulously. Start with having an awareness of the potential of corporate finance for small business and use those applications which have relevance to your business.

Key points to remember

- Corporate finance techniques which can be applied to a small private business include:
  - access to working capital;
  - valuation of the business;
  - provision of capital structure
  - acquisition, merger or trade sale initiatives;
  - shareholder management;
  - risk management.
- Sources of finance can be treated as seed capital (start-up) or operating capital (new or established business).
- The two main approaches to raising capital are equity (shareholding) and loans.
- Start-up or early-stage companies generally prefer loan equity as their businesses may have a lower value than a more established business.
- Sources of capital available to a small, private business include:
  - banks;
  - friends and family;

- business angels (high net worth individuals);
- government grants;
- own cash reserves;
- credit cards.

■ Mergers and acquisitions can be used by the SME to:
  - improve sales or profits;
  - reduce operating costs;
  - achieve growth;
  - exit from the company (partially or in full).

■ Every company should have a shareholder strategy, which includes a dividend policy, to ensure that management, directors and shareholders are agreed on the objectives of the company. The use of retained profits, specifically, should be agreed between the parties.

■ A risk strategy should include a clear path to risk management, which is a four-step process:
  - Identify the risks.
  - Assess the risks.
  - Prioritise the risks.
  - Control the risks.

■ Advisers are an essential part of most corporate finance activities. Beware – they don't come cheap, so be sure of your objectives before initiating any corporate finance activity.

12

Exit

Upon setting up a company, small business owners should have some idea of their exit strategy. This initial exit strategy in the business plan should address the owner's objectives in terms of what they hope to gain personally from the business and when.

It is not considered presumptive to do this as the exit strategy can, and often does, impact on operational decisions from the beginning and throughout the life of a company. For example, a company that was set up to provide the owner with a good income over many years may differ in its strategic and operational objectives from a business with an aggressive three-year exit plan.

Relationships with key stakeholders (as covered in Chapter 1) may be approached differently, as will some contracts such as building and leases. A company with a short-term exit plan is unlikely to want to enter into a 10-year lease, whereas a company set up to run over 20 years may be happy to do so. So, if you don't have an exit strategy now, think about what you want from this company and how it is likely to provide it to you.

Why would you want to exit?

Not all SME owners are looking for an exit. For those who do not wish to exit, there are two options. One option is to grow the company and retain ownership and, in most cases, the management of the company, while overseeing the development of the strategy. The company growth would then continue organically (through internal expansion) or through acquisition with the objective of expanding market share and perhaps product range.

The other option, which many SME owners are happy to take, is to grow the company to a level that provides the owner with a good level of income through salary and dividends. Dividends are cash payments to the shareholders from a surplus of cash, generally resulting from profits. When the company can provide this level of financial reward to its shareholders, the focus shifts from growth to maintaining a desired level of market share and profitability in order to support the cash requirement of the shareholders. For many, a lifestyle in terms of income and work/life balance is the main focus, and provided the company works to provide this, an exit strategy is not required.

If, however, you have ambitions beyond your current SME, you should consider options for an exit. An exit plan can be motivated by many factors – money, prestige, perception of success, the desire to do something new and different or a change in circumstances. Whatever the motivation, consider what your exit objectives are and monitor any changes that may occur to alter these objectives as it is this goal that will drive your company's exit strategy.

So, if you have established that an exit from the company will provide the desired outcome to meet your objectives, there are three key points that the SME owner should establish. First, the methods of exit available should be reviewed in detail. A valuation should then be investigated based on market conditions and a range of values should be decided upon. Finally, there are a range of other factors to consider, such as the impact of an exit by key shareholders.

Methods of exit

Trade sale to financiers

Often the simplest way to exit from a private company is to sell to an individual, consortium or institution who will buy all or some of the equity of the business. The contact can be instigated by you or by the acquiring party as these financiers will be keeping an eye out for companies that will be a profitable investment. Business networks and maintaining a high, positive industry profile will open doors to institutional investors or acquirers.

Trade sale to competitor

Just as you should always keep your eye on your competitors, they should be aware of your business and how you are performing. If competing companies could offer the market a better or cheaper product, there could be financial benefit from selling your company to your competitor. Companies within industries often consolidate to deter new entrants to the market, which quite often strengthens their own market position. It is quite common practice for mergers or acquisitions to occur among competing entities.

Go public

Private company shares are not tradable on the open market and therefore it is impossible to exit a limited liability company by selling a portion or all of one's shareholding to the public and more difficult to do so with an institutional investor. Private companies can become publicly traded companies by obtaining their own listing on the stock exchange, though this can mean a lot of regulation and paperwork and would only be advised if the company meets certain criteria.

Management buyout (MBO)

Sell the company to your management team. Quite often managers feel that they can unlock greater business potential, which they feel can be achieved by taking over the strategic direction themselves. If considering an exit, your answer may be sitting in the next room. It is generally the case that your management team, should they wish to carry out an MBO, will require assistance with their financing, so there is likely to be a third party, such as a financier or bank, involved in the transaction.

Brought-in management buyout (BIMBO)

In a brought-in management buyout scenario, an external management team is brought in, either by a financier or they can often be self-financed, to run and manage the company without the requirement of the existing management. It is not unusual for the BIMBO team to require a handover from existing management and therefore a 'golden handcuff' situation may be offered whereby management are retained with the promise of a bonus once the handover has been successfully concluded.

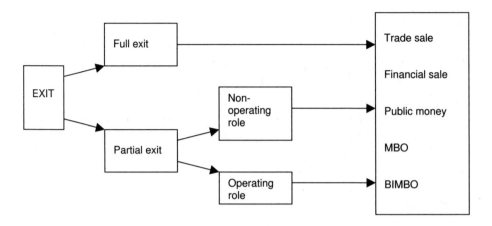

Figure 12.1   Exit methods

Exit options

One of the main decisions you will need to make is: do you wish to sell all of your shares? If the answer is yes, you are looking for a full exit; if you wish to retain some shareholding in the company going forward, you seek a partial exit.

You then should consider whether or not you wish to have any interaction or active role within the company after your exit. Whether or not you wish to have an operating role in the company will affect the detail of the exit and potentially the parties available to you as some, such as a competitor purchaser, may require a full exit and non-operating role from shareholders and perhaps directors.

While the outcome options are the same regardless of which path the business owner takes (Figure 12.1), the complexity within the outcome will be very different, so it is worth deciding which of the above courses best suits your requirements from the exit.

So, which of these options is likely to be best for you and your company? You will need to carry out financial analysis to ensure that you are making the best deal for you and your shareholders, while maintaining your fiduciary duties to your employees and other stakeholders.

Case study

The directors of TravelCo wanted to approach their parent company about a management buyout. The directors felt that the group in which they operated placed unreasonable constraints on the operations of their subsidiary business, which were holding it back in terms of competitive advantage, resulting in a lower market share, sales and profits.

Not having the required capital to fund the buyout themselves, they approached a series of business angels (high net worth individuals) to try to obtain financial backing. It was difficult to convince an external third party that they could make the company more profitable if was removed from the large international group in which it then operated. After a series of unsuccessful pitches to potential investors, they decided to approach the parent company with the proposal of an 'earn out' scenario.

The proposal consisted of a valuation of the business as a stand-alone entity, which would be paid for using a small proportion of cash. They would pay the balance of the price with a percentage of profits over a fixed period. This way, the directors could obtain 100 per cent of the shareholding of the company and be free to operate it as they wished. The plan succeeded. Two years after the management buyout was achieved, the directors went on to sell a high proportion of the company to a competitor at a considerable benefit to themselves financially. It was a high-risk strategy as they had to support the working capital from retained profits, while running a lean operation without the support of a global group. While their strategy changed from wanting to own their own company to achieving a trade sale just two years later, the directors saw the corporate finance activity as a success.

Company valuation

Once the business owner has an idea of the method which the exit transaction is likely to take, it is important to value the company. When setting out to make the decision as to how and when to exit your company, a business owner should carry out basic financial valuation analysis to obtain a sensible and realistic range of valuations of the company.

Be realistic about the value of your business. There are many ways to value a business and it's likely that whatever method you or the other parties involved in the transaction choose, your business valuation is likely to be lower than you hoped.

There are many theoretic methods to value a company; however, in practice there are three main valuation methods used in today's corporate finance market, which are used for both trade and financial purchases.

Valuation method 1: comparable public companies

Public transactions have a much greater level of transparency than private companies, so you can gain access to information such as the valuation and what was actually paid for the company. There should be full disclosure on the components of the deal, which will enable an analysis to be carried out on the structure and financial position of the company. This is useful if using the transaction as a basis for a private company valuation.

Public companies generally sell for a greater valuation, based on higher multiples of turnover or profits than a private company, so any valuation taken from a public company transaction should be reduced accordingly. The amount of the reduction will depend on market conditions and the financial health of both companies.

Valuation method 2: comparable transactions

Keep an eye on what is happening with your competitors and other companies operating within your industry. The market conditions within the industry are shared by all who operate within that environment, so financiers will often be comfortable valuing a private company by comparing recent transactions within the same operating environment as the company looking for a sale.

Read the trade press, talk to suppliers and customers and try to gain as much information as possible. You want to know about the sale value and ideally what was involved in the deal, ie whether it was all cash, partial earn-out etc. Any information that can be gained from similar transactions will be a good basis from which to negotiate a valuation for the company.

Valuation method 3: discounted cashflow (DCF)

The discounted cashflow (DCF) method is the most common method used by bankers, corporate financiers and independent purchasers. While it may not be the basis of a final agreed valuation, it is most certainly a calculation that will be carried out in the course of exit negotiations, so it is worthwhile being comfortable with how a DCF calculation works.

The component parts required for the calculation are as follows:

1. cashflow forecast, either 12 or 24 months, whichever is more appropriate for your business and the transaction;
2. rate of interest paid on current debt – 'cost of debt';
3. the minimum rate of return expected by shareholders, which has been agreed by the company – 'cost of equity'.

Now, put the cost of debt and cost of equity together to create a weighted average cost of capital (WACC) figure that will be used in the final DCF formula. The WACC formula will provide the capital structure of the company and can be calculated as follows:

$$Q = (1 - x)\, Ye + xZ$$

where:

Q = the weighted average cost of capital (WACC) for the company
x = the debt to equity ratio, which is calculated as $D / (D + E)$
Y = the cost of equity
Z = the post-tax cost of debt
D = the market value of the company's debt, including loans from banks and other financial institutions
E = the market value of all equity.

Or the formula can be stated as:

WACC = (1 – debt to capital ratio) × cost of equity + debt to capital ratio × cost of debt

Discounted cashflow can be carried out using the following equation. This is a simplified model based on one cashflow in one future period:

$$DCF = \left(\frac{FV}{(1+d)^n} \right)$$

where:

DCF is the discounted present value of future cashflows (FV)
FV is the nominal value of a cashflow amount in a future period – use the information from your cashflow forecast
d is the WACC
n is the number of discounting periods used (the period in which the future cashflow occurs). For example, if used a 12-month cashflow forecast as the basis for the FV, then $n = 1$ (1 year), if used 24 months, then $n = 2$ (2 years) and so on.

DCF – practical example of use for a trade sale

The director and majority shareholder of Exit Ltd is looking for an exit from the small company which he started five years ago. He is looking to sell 100 per cent of his shareholding, as are the remaining shareholders. None of the parties wish an ongoing role in the company.

After reviewing their options, they have been approached by a competitor who wishes to begin trade sale negotiations. The director, therefore, carries out a valuation of his company by way of a discounted cashflow calculation.

The directors have prepared a cashflow forecast for the next 12 months, which shows turnover of £1m and pre-tax profit of £100,000. The balance sheet shows a total current debt figure of £200,000 and total equity of £750,000.

The post-tax cost of the debt is 5 per cent and the company pays shareholders a 10 per cent return on their investment in the company.

Applying these figures to the above formula, the component parts read as follows:

$$Q = (1 - x)\, Ye + xZ$$

where:

Q = the weighted average cost of capital (WACC)
x = £200,000 / (£200,000 + £750,000) = 0.21
Y = 10%

Z = 5%
D = £200,000
E = £750,000

therefore, $Q = (1-.21).1+.21*.05$

The total of Q, being the WACC, is 0.9005.

Take the turnover of the projected cashflows for the next 12 months and multiply this figure by the WACC:

£1,000,000 × 0.9005 = £900,500

The valuation that can be placed on the company is £900,500.

This method should be appropriate for any small, private company to value their business. The output from the application of the formula should be used as a starting point for negotiations with a third party.

Other factors to consider on exit

Ensure that all relevant parties have been considered. The directors of a company have a responsibility to consider the needs of certain stakeholders and must ensure that their decision takes the needs and legal obligations of these parties into consideration.

Employees have rights that a company must uphold. If selling the company on to a third party, the employees will need to know if they will have future employment under the new ownership. This can sometimes be a very complex area and it is worth investigating all areas of responsibility to ensure that you are meeting your legal obligations where employees are concerned.

It is advisable at this point to seek legal advice to ensure that you are able to carry out the desired exit plan within the structure of your company and that of the other party.

Conclusion

An exit won't suit everyone, but if you think an exit may be an option, it is important to have an exit strategy and apply this, where possible, to the overall strategy of the business.

The SME owner who is looking for a potential exit from the company should also have an awareness and preferably a working knowledge of the techniques covered in this chapter in terms of company valuation and methods of exit. Knowledge in this area can add real value to financial negotiations with a potential acquirer of the business.

Key points to remember

- Do you need an exit strategy?
- Why would you want to exit your company?
- Methods of exit:
  - Trade sale to financiers.
  - Trade sale to competitor.
  - Go public – list on a stock exchange to increase the liquidity of your shares.
  - Management buyout (MBO) – the management of the company buy the company from the existing shareholders with a view of continuing to manage the operations.
  - Brought-in management buyout (BIMBO) – an external management team is brought in with a view of buying the company from the existing shareholders and then taking over the operations from the existing management team.
- Company valuation – three methods:
  - comparable public company valuations;
  - comparable transaction values and deal structure;
  - discounted cashflow (DCF) calculation.

Glossary

Accruals   The accounting method of recognising an expense in the accounting period that is not yet received by invoice or other documentation. Accruals are integral to the matching principle of accounting.

Amortisation   Depreciation relating to intangible assets.

Brainstorming   Starting with a blank page, note down every idea that comes to mind about the given topic. It is often useful to have parties with different experience and focus for this exercise.

Business angels   High net worth individuals who invest their own or consortium money in companies. They will often expect some input into management, such as a board seat, though some business angels wish to remain silent.

Consistency   Reliability or uniformity. One of the four basic accounting fundamentals.

Contingency planning   Plan B.

Corporate governance   The duties of the statutory directors of a company. It is the framework in which the company is operated and regulated from a legal point of view that provides its corporate governance.

Cost of capital   Sum of the cost of debt and the cost of equity.

Dividends   Money paid to the shareholders of a company from retained profits after the year end. Shareholders will normally require a dividend policy to be agreed prior to investment.

EBITDA   Earnings before interest, tax, depreciation and amortisation. A figure used on a profit and loss statement to provide analysis of trading profit.

Entrepreneurial   The spirit of a person who takes risks associated with turning opportunity into profit.

Fixed costs   Fixed costs are a constant expense of the business and do not fluctuate with business activity.

Forward analysis   Using historical or current data to forecast or predict future behaviour or performance.

Goal congruence   When two parties have the same goals and objectives when operating either independently or jointly, they are said to have goal congruence. It is simply a meeting of minds that is often critical for good business behaviour.

Going concern   When a company can pay its debts as and when they fall due (liquidity), it is considered a going concern. If a company is illiquid, it must justify how it will continue to trade out of this position.

KPIs   Key performance indicators. Metrics upon which the company measures financial performance.

Liquid   A company is liquid when it can pay its debts as and when they fall due. Current assets should be greater than current liabilities.

Liquidation   A company can be put into liquidation when it is no longer considered a going concern.

Matching   To ensure that costs are matched in the period in which the related sales are recognised. Accruals are the best way to ensure matching in the accounts. One of the four basic accounting fundamentals.

Organic growth   Company growth that is generated internally, such as a new sales office opened using retained profits.

Overheads   Overheads are expenses which cannot be directly apportioned to trading activity, such as rent or administrative expenses.

Planning horizon   A relevant and appropriate period for which a company performs a planning or budgeting activity.

Probability analysis   The calculation of the likelihood of an event based on previous experience and management assumptions.

Prudence   Caution or a reluctance to take risks. One of the four basic accounting fundamentals.

Quantitative analysis   The collection and reporting of financial data.

Retained profits   Profits after tax, depreciation and amortisation. Cash from retained profits can be used as the dividend pool or for further investment.

Role congruence   An absence of conflict between the role of the employee in terms of the company and their own personal moral code or professional conduct requirements.

SME   Small to medium-sized enterprise. Refer to the introduction of this book for the quantified parameters of each size of company as laid down by the government.

Solvency   Solvency is a company that is liquid, ie that a company can pay its debts as and when they fall due.

Sunk costs   Costs that have already been incurred are called sunk costs and should not factor into any decision-making activity regarding a current or future opportunity.

Variable costs   Variable costs are expenses that change with the level of operations of the business. They differ from fixed costs, such as rent, which remains constant regardless of output units in a period.

Further reading

BPP Publishing (2001) *Management Accounting – Decision Making*, BPP Publishing, London

BPP Publishing (2002) *Management Accounting – Business Strategy*, BPP Publishing, London

BPP Publishing (2002) *Management Accounting – Financial Strategy*, BPP Publishing, London

BPP Publishing (2002) *Management Accounting – Information Strategy*, BPP Publishing, London

Brealey, R and Myers, S (2000) *Principles of Corporate Finance*, McGraw-Hill, New York

Elangovan, A (2001) Causal ordering of stress, satisfaction and commitment, and intention to quit: a structural equations analysis, *Leadership & Organizational Development Journal*, **22** (4), pp 159–65

Fletcher, B and Jones, F (1992) Measuring organisational culture, the cultural audit, *Managerial Auditing Journal*, **7** (6), pp 30–36

Hofstede, G (1990) Measuring organisational culture, a qualitative and quantitative study across twenty cases, *Administrative Science Quarterly*, **35** (21), pp 286–317

Maitland, I (1996) *Successful Business Plans*, Hodder and Stoughton, London

Saunders, M, Lewis, P and Thornhill, A (2003) *Research Methods for Business Students*, Pearson Education, Essex

Silbiger, S (1993) *The 10 Day MBA*, William Morrow and Company, New York

Index

NB: page numbers in *italic* indicate figures or tables